Michael Macfarlane

OFFICE MATTERS
Englisch für kaufmännische Büroberufe

Anja Wenk
Tonnaer Straße 02
99947 Bad Langensalza
Telefon 0 36 03 / 81 20 67

OFFICE MATTERS – Englisch für kaufmännische Büroberufe
wurde geplant und entwickelt von der Verlagsredaktion Cornelsen & Oxford University Press GmbH, Berlin.
Das Lehrwerk wurde verfasst von Michael Macfarlane, Oxford in Zusammenarbeit mit David Clarke, Witten.

Beratende Mitarbeit:	Jürgen Telle, Goslar
	Hans-Werner Maier, Landshut
	Angela Elsner, München
Verlagsredaktion:	James Abram, Salzburg;
	James Austin,
	Simon Caridia
Gestaltung und Herstellung:	Marc Berger

Erhältlich sind auch:
Cassette (Best.-Nr. 22480)
Lehrerhandbuch (Best.-Nr. 22489)

1. Auflage ✔
    98   99   00   2001   Die ersten Ziffern bezeichnen
    4.   5.   6.   7.   Zahl und Jahr des Druckes.

Alle Drucke dieser Auflage können, weil untereinander unverändert,
im Unterricht nebeneinander verwendet werden.

BESTELLNUMMER **22471**

© Cornelsen & Oxford University Press GmbH, Berlin, 1995
Das Werk und seine Teile sind urheberrechtlich geschützt.
Jede Verwertung in anderen als den gesetzlich zugelassenen Fällen
bedarf deshalb der vorherigen schriftlichen Einwilligung des Verlages.

ISBN 3-8109-2247-1

Reproduktion	Schütte & Behling, Berlin
Druck / Weiterverarbeitung:	Saladruck
Vertrieb:	Cornelsen Verlag, Berlin

Gedruckt auf chlorfrei gebleichtem Papier ohne Dioxinbelastung der Gewässer.

Vorwort

OFFICE MATTERS ist ein einbändiges Englisch-Lehrwerk für Fachklassen, die die Ausbildung zum Bürokaufmann / zur Bürokauffrau bzw. zum Kaufmann / zur Kauffrau für Bürokommunikation absolvieren. Es eignet sich auch zum Einsatz in Kursen mit ähnlichen Zielsetzungen. Es setzt nur geringe Englischkenntnisse voraus.

Das Lehrwerk enthält drei Abschnitte, die jeweils aus fünf Units, Correspondence und zwei Tests bestehen:
1. Abschnitt – *Units* 1-5; *Correspondence* A, *Test* 1/2
2. Abschnitt – *Units* 6-10; *Correspondence* B, *Test* 3/4
3. Abschnitt – *Units* 11-15; *Correspondence* C, *Test* 5/6

Die *Units* 1–15 sind wie folgt aufgebaut:
- *Warm up:* Erster Einstieg in das jeweilige Thema durch Bilder und Aufgaben;
- *People at work:* Dialog mit stark berufsbezogenem Inhalt, dazu Verständnisfragen, Wortschatzarbeit und Grammatikübungen;
- *English at work:* Aufgaben, die speziell die Kommunikation mit und unter den Lernenden anregen;
- *Over to you:* Aufgaben, die eine freie mündliche Umsetzung des Gelernten ermöglichen;
- *Focus on grammar:* Kurze Regelerklärungen auf Deutsch.

Die drei *Correspondence*-Einheiten enthalten folgende Komponenten:
- Musterbriefe bzw. -faxe, die Gestaltung und Inhalt von verschiedenen Briefformen veranschaulichen;
- Verständnisfragen zu den Musterbriefen;
- Aufgaben, die anhand angegebener Textbausteine gelöst werden können.

Es wird empfohlen, die *Correspondence* nach den *Units* des Abschnitts durchzuarbeiten.

- ◘◘ = Dialoge bzw. Texte, die Sie auf der Cassette finden.
- ◘ = Beispielsatz
- ◘ = Vorsicht!

Inhaltsverzeichnis

1. Abschnitt

6	Unit 1	**The first day**

Begrüßen • sich und andere vorstellen • Berufsbezeichnungen
Das Verb to be • Wochentage • Monate • Ordnungszahlen • Datum • Pronomen und besitzanzeigende Adjektive • das simple present (1) • Adverbien der Häufigkeit • adverbiale Bestimmungen

14	Unit 2	**Getting started**

Bezeichnungen für Bürogeräte • sagen und fragen, wo sich bestimmte Abteilungen befinden
Präpositionen • Mengenbezeichnungen (some, any) • this/these, that/those • das simple present (2)

22	Unit 3	**An urgent order**

Die Struktur einer Firma • eine Laufbahn beschreiben
Adverbiale Bestimmungen der Zeit • unbestimmter Artikel a/an • das simple past: to be • das simple past: regelmäßige Verben

30	Unit 4	**Computers**

Der Computerarbeitsplatz • einen Computer bedienen
Die modalen Hilfsverben: can/could (was able to), must, needn't, may

38	Unit 5	**A visitor**

Sich um einen Besucher kümmern
Futur mit will • would • Subjektfragen mit who und what

46	Test 1/2	

2. Abschnitt

48	Unit 6	**Changing jobs**

Verkaufszahlen beschreiben • über Fähigkeiten und Vorlieben reden
Das modale Hilfsverb should

56	Unit 7	**An order**

Telefonieren (1)
Das Alphabet und der Buchstabiercode • das present continuous • das simple present und present continuous im Vergleich

64	Unit 8	**Delivering goods**

Transportformen • Telefonieren (2)
Adjektive und Adverbien • Steigerung der Adjektive

72	Unit 9	**A surprise**

Die Uhrzeit • Fahrpläne • Telefonieren (3)
Das present perfect • Zusammensetzungen mit some, any, every, no

80	Unit 10	**Going home**

Verkaufszahlen • Telefonieren (4)
Das simple past und present perfect im Vergleich • das present continuous mit zukünftiger Bedeutung

88	Test 3/4	

3. Abschnitt

90   **Unit 11**   **Back in Munich**
Nach dem Weg fragen / den Weg beschreiben •
über die eigene Arbeit reden
Verben mit dem Gerundium (ing-Form) oder Infinitiv

98   **Unit 12**   **A trip abroad**
Reisen buchen und umbuchen • Telefonieren (5)
If-Sätze (Typ 1) • Das simple present bei Fahrplänen

106   **Unit 13**   **A complaint**
Probleme beschreiben • firmeninterne Abläufe beschreiben •
Telefonieren (6)
*So und not im Anschluss an ein Verb • who, which, that •
one of, some of, most, usw.*

114   **Unit 14**   **The conference**
Eine Besprechung organisieren • Telefonieren (7)
*Be going to mit zukünftiger Bedeutung • höfliche Bitten mit could •
too und (not) enough*

122   **Unit 15**   **A new job**
Speisekarten
Unregelmäßige Verben

130   **Test 5/6**

Correspondence

132   **A**   **Types of business letter**
An enquiry • a request for a quotation • an offer • an order

139   **B**   **Form and layout**
A business letter • a fax

149   **C**   **Complaints and reminders**
*A complaint about a delay in delivery • a reply to a complaint about a delay
in delivery • a complaint about wrong goods • a reply to a complaint about
wrong goods • a reminder • a reply to a reminder*

Anhang

158   **I**   **Pairwork Files**
164   **II**   **Chronologisches Wörterverzeichnis**
176   **III**   **Alphabetisches Wörterverzeichnis**
186   **IV**   **Grundwortschatz**

1 The first day — Warm-up

MEMO MEMO MEMO
von: System 7 GmbH, Munich
an: System 7 (UK) Ltd, Oxford
Datum: 24 September
Betreff: Visit of trainees from head office

Dear Mrs Reece

This is to confirm the visit of two trainees: Petra Hoffmann and Dieter Salter.
They arrive at London Heathrow on 1 October (flight LH 4192 from Munich).

With best wishes
Peter Schliemann
Peter Schliemann
(Personnel Manager)

1 Complete the sentences.

1 The young people in the picture are from … . (country)
2 His name is … and her name is … .
3 They are trainees with … . (company)
4 Their flight is from … to … . (airports)

People at work

The trainees from Munich

System 7 GmbH is a large European producer of office furniture. The company has sales offices in France, Spain and the UK, and a factory in Britain too. Petra Hoffmann and Dieter Salter are trainees at System 7's head office in Munich. All new trainees learn about other parts of the organization.

Petra and Dieter are now on a visit to System 7 (UK) Ltd in Oxford. This is their first morning. The assistant personnel manager Mike Parker meets them at their hotel.

MIKE	Excuse me. Are you the new trainees from Munich?
PETRA	Yes, we are.
DIETER	That's right.
MIKE	Well, good morning. I'm Mike Parker.
DIETER	I'm Dieter Salter. Good morning.
PETRA	And my name is Petra Hoffmann.
MIKE	Pleased to meet you. … Tell me, is your hotel all right?
DIETER	Yes, it's fine, thanks.
PETRA	And the food is very good.

MIKE	Here we are. Now come and meet my boss, Lucy Reece. She's in charge of personnel. … Lucy, this is Petra Hoffmann and this is Dieter Salter. Petra, Dieter – Lucy Reece.
BOTH	How do you do, Mrs Reece?
LUCY	Oh, please don't call me Mrs Reece. Just call me Lucy. We're very informal here.

MIKE	Next, let's look around the factory.
DIETER	It's quite big.
MIKE	Yes, about 200 people work here. Ah, look. That's Jameel Patel over there.
PETRA	What does he do?
MIKE	He runs the factory. He's the production manager. Let's go and talk to him.

People at work

2 Match the questions and answers.

1 Where is System 7's head office? A Jameel Patel
2 Who is the assistant personnel manager? B personnel manager
3 What is Lucy Reece's job? C about 200
4 What is the production manager's name? D Mike Parker
5 How many people are there in production? E Munich

3 Complete the sentences with these words.

factory • manager • office • sales • trainees

1 I work in this … . That's my desk over there.
2 Petra and Dieter are two … from head office.
3 About 200 people work in System 7's … in Oxford.
4 Jack works in … . He sells his company's products all over Europe.
5 Alan is a … now. He's in charge of 25 people.

4 Work with a partner. Complete the dialogues. Then practise them.

I • me • my • them • they • we • you • your

AT A TRADE FAIR:

REED   Hello. I'm Peter Reed. …'m¹ with EBM.
HALL   Pleased to meet …². …³ name is Alison Hall.
REED   …⁴ products look good, and …'re⁵ not too expensive.
HALL   Thank you. Come and look at …⁶ with …⁷. Perhaps …⁸ can do business.

To be	I **am** (I**'m**)	he **is** (he**'s**)	we **are** (we**'re**)
	you **are** (you**'re**)	she **is** (she**'s**)	they **are** (they**'re**)
		it **is** (it**'s**)	

are (3x) • 'm (2x) • 's

A FEW WEEKS LATER AT EBM:

BRANT   Good afternoon. I…⁹ Lisa Brant. …¹⁰ you Alison Hall?
HALL   That…¹¹ right.
BRANT   Mr Reed and his colleagues …¹² ready to see you now. Please come this way.

REED   Hello. Nice to see you again! How …¹³ you?
HALL   I…¹⁴ very well, thanks. You too?
REED   Fine, thanks. Now come in and meet the others.

Greeting people

Greeting people for the first time
Hello. My name is (Mike Parker). How do you do?
Hello. I'm (Petra Hoffmann). How do you do?

Good morning. I'm (Mike Parker). Are you (Dieter Salter)?
Yes, that's right. Pleased to meet you.

(Good afternoon: *12 a.m. – 5.30 p.m.*)
(Good evening: *5.30 p.m. – 10 p.m.*)

Greeting people you know
Hello, (Alison)! Nice to see you again. How are you?
Hi! *(informal)* I'm very well, thanks, (Peter). How are you?

Introducing people
Hello, (Lucy). This is (Petra Hoffmann) from Munich.
How do you do?
Pleased to meet you.

Saying goodbye
Goodbye. 'Bye. *(informal)*
Goodnight. *(5.30 p.m. – 12 p.m.)*

5 What can you say in English when …

1. you greet somebody formally for the first time?
2. you are pleased to meet somebody?
3. you greet somebody you have met before?
4. you greet somebody in the afternoon?
5. you say goodbye at the end of the day?

Practise these phrases with a partner. Use your own names.

Now introduce your partner to someone else in the class.

6 Give the missing words.

1. Petra and Dieter *work for* System 7 in Munich. (work for / works for)
2. Petra *comes from* a small town near Munich. (come from / comes from)
3. Dieter … System 7 in Munich. (work for / works for)
4. Dieter's mother and father still … Hamburg. (live in / lives in)
5. Mike Parker and Lucy Reece … trainees from head office. (look after / looks after)
6. About 200 people … the factory. (work in / works in)

English at work

7 Match the people and their jobs. Then make complete sentences.

William James is the mailroom supervisor. He deals with the company's mail.

1	a receptionist	A	does the filing
2	the mailroom supervisor	B	welcomes visitors to the company
3	a trainee	C	deals with the company's mail
4	the assistant personnel manager	D	learns about different jobs
5	a secretary	E	types Lucy's and Mike's letters and reports
6	a clerk	F	helps with staff pay and conditions
7	the personnel manager	G	looks after staff pay and conditions

8 Look at Exercise 7 again and correct these sentences.

1 Jean Glass is the mailroom supervisor.
No, she isn't. She's a receptionist.
2 Sally Hines is the assistant personnel manager.
3 Mike Parker is a filing clerk.
4 Rob Bennett is a secretary.
5 Jane Stevens is the personnel manager.
6 William James is a trainee.
7 Lucy Reece is a receptionist.

What's your job? What do you do at work every day?

I'm a secretary. I type letters and reports.

9 Work with a partner.
Read what Jane Stevens says and put the pictures (A–G) in order (1–7).

1 = C

"I always start work at 8.30. First I check the fax machine. Then Lucy and I talk about the day's work, and we always check her diary together. The mail usually arrives at 9.30, so then I open the letters and I give them to Lucy and Mike. After that I usually type letters and reports.

I stop and have lunch at 1 o'clock. Then in the afternoon, I do various things. For example, I check the stationery cupboard once or twice a week. And I order a list of new things from stationery stores – paper, envelopes and so on. At the end of the day I usually go home at 5 o'clock."

10 Correct the sentences.

1 Jane sometimes starts work at 8.30.
   No, she doesn't. She always starts work at 8.30.
2 The mail usually arrives after 9.30.
3 Lucy and Jane always check Ann's diary.
4 Lucy and Mike open the letters.
5 Jane sometimes types letters and reports.
6 She orders new stationery three times a week.
7 She usually goes home before 5 o'clock.

Days of the week
Monday	Tuesday	Wednesday	Thursday	Friday	Saturday	Sunday
(Mon)	(Tues)	(Wed)	(Thurs)	(Fri)	(Sat)	(Sun)

Months
January	February	March	April	May	June
(Jan)	(Feb)	(Mar)	(Apr)	(May)	(Jun)
July	August	September	October	November	December
(Jul)	(Aug)	(Sept)	(Oct)	(Nov)	(Dec)

Over to you

11 Work with a partner. Read about Petra and Dieter.
Then complete their record cards for personnel.

Petra Hoffmann and Dieter Salter are trainees at System 7. She is in marketing and he is in purchasing. They are the same age and their dates of birth are nearly the same too. Her date of birth is 21st January, 1977, and his date of birth is just two weeks after that.

Family name ... 1	Family name Hoffmann
First name ... 2	First name ... 5
Company position ... 3	Company position marketing trainee
Date of birth ... 4	Date of birth ... 6

Write your own record card.

Make sentences like these:
My full name is …
I'm a/an …
I'm … years old.
My date of birth is …

Now write your partner's record card.

Ask questions like these:
What's your (family name), please?
How old are you?

Now ask about other people:
What's his/her (family name)? How old is he/she?

Ordinal numbers

1st – first	9th – ninth	17th – seventeenth
2nd – second	10th – tenth	18th – eighteenth
3rd – third	11th – eleventh	19th – nineteenth
4th – fourth	12th – twelfth	20th – twentieth
5th – fifth	13th – thirteenth	21st – twenty-first
6th – sixth	14th – fourteenth	…
7th – seventh	15th – fifteenth	30th – thirtieth
8th – eighth	16th – sixteenth	31st – thirty-first

Dates

You can ask:	You can answer:	You can also say:
What's the date (today)?	It's the first of April. (It's 1st April.)	It's Monday, the first of April, 19… .
What date is it (today)?	It's April the first. (It's April 1st.)	

Focus on grammar

A. Pronouns and possessive adjectives
(Pronomen und besitzanzeigende Adjektive)

SUBJECT PRONOUNS	I	you	he/she/it	we	they
OBJECT PRONOUNS	**me**	**you**	**him/her/it**	**us**	**them**
POSSESSIVE ADJECTIVES	**my**	**your**	**his/her/its**	**our**	**their**

❗ **He, she** *bei Personen;* **it** *bei Gegenständen.*

> *Unterscheiden Sie zwischen:*
> your   you're (= you are)   his   he's (= he is / he has)
> its   it's (= it is / it has)   their   they're (= they are)

B. Simple present (1) *(die einfache Gegenwart)*

TO HAVE		OTHER VERBS	
I have (**I've**)	he **has** (he**'s**)	I work	he work**s**
you have (you**'ve**)	she **has** (she**'s**)	you work	she work**s**
we have (we**'ve**)	it **has** (it**'s**)	we work	it work**s**
they have (they**'ve**)		they work	

Man verwendet das **simple present** *für*
- *eine wiederholte oder regelmäßige Handlung, z.B.* He **runs** the factory.
- *einen Zustand/Vorgang von Dauer, z.B.* Petra and Dieter **are** trainees at System 7.

❗ *Verb* + **-s** *nach* **he**, **she** *und* **it**.

C. Frequency *(Häufigkeit)*

ADVERBS *(Adverbien)*		TIME PHRASES *(adverbiale Bestimmungen)*	
always	*immer*	once/twice	an hour
usually	*normalerweise*	twice	a day
normally	*normalerweise*	three times	a week
often	*oft*	several times	a month
sometimes	*manchmal*	in the	morning
hardly ever	*kaum*		afternoon
never	*niemals*	every	day/Friday
			month/year

> *Merken Sie sich den Unterschied bei der Wortstellung im Satz:*
> I **always** cycle to work.
> I   cycle to work **every day**.

2 Getting started — Warm-up

1 Mike and Dieter are in Dieter's new office.
Match the desk equipment (1-12) to the illustrations (A-L).

1. ruler ✓
2. pencils ✗
3. calculator ✓
4. biros ✓
5. desk lamp ✗
6. stapler ✓
7. staples ✗
8. hole punch ✗
9. files ✓
10. paper clips ✗
11. notepad ✗
12. wastepaper bin ✓

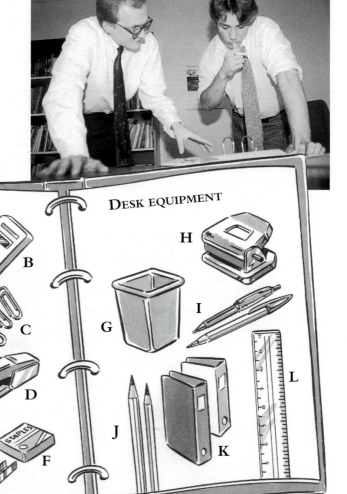

2 Work with a partner. Look at the list in Exercise 1 and ask and answer questions.

Is there a (ruler)?   *Yes, there is. / No, there isn't.*
Does Dieter have any (pencils)?   *Yes, he does. / No, he doesn't.*

People at work

Petra's desk

MIKE   OK, we're on the first floor now, and this is your office. Room 101.
PETRA Is this my desk here?
MIKE   No, it's that one over there in the corner.

MIKE   You need a staff phone list, Petra. Here you are.
PETRA Thanks.
MIKE   Here's your name and your room number. Look.
PETRA And is this my extension number?
MIKE   Yes, that's it. You're on extension 607.

MIKE   Now let's check your other desk equipment.
PETRA One problem. There isn't a desk lamp.
MIKE   Right. One desk lamp. … Next, is there a calculator?
PETRA I don't know.
MIKE   Check that drawer on the left. Is it in there?
PETRA Yes, that's right. It's here in the drawer.

MIKE   OK, what's next on the list? Do you have a stapler?
PETRA Yes, I do. But I don't have any staples.
MIKE   Right, so you need some staples.
PETRA Tell me, where do I go for new equipment?
MIKE   To the stationery store in the mailroom. That's on the ground floor.

3 Answer the questions.

1. Which floor is Petra's office on?
2. What does Mike give her?
3. Is there a desk lamp on her desk?
4. Where is the calculator?
5. Does she have a stapler and staples?

People at work

4 Work with a partner. Ask and answer questions about the picture.

in • on • on the left/right • next to • under

*Where's the wastepaper bin?
It's under the desk.*

5 Work with a partner. Complete the dialogues. Then practise them.

this • that • these • those

MIKE   Come in, Dieter. Here's your new office.
DIETER Thanks. Is ...¹ my desk here by the door?
MIKE   No. ...'s² your desk over there under the window.
DIETER Ah, right. And are ...³ things on the desk for me?
MIKE   Yes, and ...⁴ files are for you too. Here you are.
MIKE   Thanks.

in • next to • on (3x) • under • with

MIKE   First, you need a staff phone list.
DIETER Mm, I don't see one ...⁵ the other things ...⁶ the desk.
MIKE   Is it ...⁷ that big file? Pick it up and look.
DIETER No, it isn't here.
MIKE   Well, look ...⁸ the drawer ...⁹ the right.
DIETER No, sorry. It's empty.
MIKE   Ah! Look! It's there ...¹⁰ the floor ...¹¹ the wastepaper bin.

Neues für den Walkman!

Textcassette

Mit diesen Texten, die von geschulten englischen und amerikanischen Sprechern gelesen werden, üben Sie Ihre Aussprache und das Hörverständnis für authentisches Englisch. Es empfiehlt sich, jeweils die Abschnitte mit Hilfe der Cassette zu bearbeiten, die gerade im Unterricht behandelt werden.

Auf der Cassette finden Sie sämtliche Lesetexte der Units.

Bitte beachten Sie auch die Rückseite dieser Karte.

Bestellkarte

Hiermit bestelle ich zur Lieferung durch Nachnahme. Preis zuzüglich Porto (ca. 3,50 DM), Nachnahmegebühr (ca. 5,— DM), Zustellgebühr (ca. 3,— DM).

☐ **Office Matters, Textcassette**
Laufzeit ca. 80 Min, Bestellnr. 22480 ◊ 31,80 DM

☐ **Business Grammar – Elementary**
Lösungsheft beigelegt, Bestellnr. 27465 19,80 DM

☐ **Business Vocabulary – Elementary**
Bestellnr. 27520 19,80 DM

Gewünschtes bitte in dem entsprechenden Kästchen deutlich ankreuzen. Alle Titel können auch durch den Buchhandel zum Ladenpreis ohne die Postgebühren bezogen werden.
Preisstand 1.1.1998. Änderungen vorbehalten. ◊ = Unverbindliche Preisempfehlung.

Business Grammar – Elementary

Probleme mit der englischen Grammatik? Dieses Übungsbuch hilft Lernenden mit geringen Vorkenntnissen, sich in der englischen Grammatik zurechtzufinden.

Es ist in 10 Units aufgeteilt und behandelt vor allem die Bereiche der Grammatik, mit denen Deutsche erfahrungsgemäß Schwierigkeiten haben.

Die Lösungen stehen in einem Extraheft, das dem Übungsbuch beiliegt. So kann man ohne fremde Hilfe kleine Wissenslücken schließen.

Business Vocabulary – Elementary

Beim letzten Vokabeltest durchgefallen? Auch dieses Übungsbuch richtet sich speziell an Lernende mit geringen Vorkenntnissen.

In sinnvollem Zusammenhang gelernte Wörter lassen sich leichter merken, deshalb ist der Grundwortschatz des *Business English* hier in thematischen Einheiten – „Wortfeldern" – präsentiert.

Zahlreiche Übungen helfen, das neue Vokabular zu festigen und man kann wieder mitreden!

Bitte in Druckschrift ausfüllen

Name / Vorname

Straße / Hausnummer

Postleitzahl / Ort

Ort / Datum

Unterschrift (ggf. des / der Erziehungsberechtigten)

Bitte freimachen

Antwortkarte

Cornelsen

Verlagskontor

33598 Bielefeld

6 Put the verbs in the correct forms.

1 Petra (✓) *needs* a desk lamp from the store, but she (✗) *doesn't need* a calculator. (need)
2 She (✓) … some staples from the store, but she (✗) … a stapler. (need)
3 Petra and Dieter (✗) … France. They (✓) … Germany. (come from)
4 Mike (✗) … in marketing. He (✓) … in personnel. (work)
5 Mike and Lucy (✓) … new trainees, but they (✗) … the monthly pay cheques. (deal with)

7 Form questions.

1 Petra (need) a desk lamp
  Does Petra need a desk lamp?
2 Mike and Lucy (work) in marketing
  Do Mike and Lucy work in marketing?
3 Petra (speak) English
4 Petra and Dieter (come from) Germany
5 Lucy and Mike (work for) System 7 in Germany
6 Lucy (deal with) pay and conditions
7 you (work for) a big organization

8 Look at Exercise 7 again. Ask and answer the questions with a partner.

Does Petra need a desk lamp? *Yes, she does.*
Do Mike and Lucy work in marketing? *No, they don't. They work in personnel.*

9 Form questions and answers. Then match the questions to the answers.

(1 = C) Where does Jane Stevens work? She works at System 7 (UK).
1 where (Jane Stevens) work
2 what (she do) at work
3 when (she start) work in the morning
4 why (she talk) to Lucy early each morning
5 how often (she check) the stationery cupboard

A she (do) that once a week
B she (start) work at 8.30
C she (work) at System 7 (UK)
D she (help) Lucy and Mike in personnel
E because she (need) to talk about the day's work

English at work

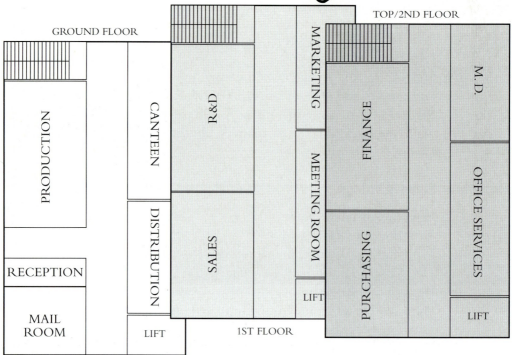

10 Say where places are.

The canteen is on the ground floor.
It's along the corridor from the lifts. It's opposite the stairs.

Giving directions (1)

| The ... is on the | 2nd/top
1st
ground | floor. | It's | next to
opposite
near | the lifts.
the stairs.
the canteen. |

| It's | along
across
at the end of | the corridor | from the lifts.
on the left.
on the right. |

11 You and Petra are on the 1st floor in the sales office. She needs directions to different places.
Work with a partner. Complete her questions and your answers.

– How do I get to the canteen, please?
– Take the lift to the ground floor. It's along the corridor from the lifts. It's opposite the stairs.

Giving directions (2)

How do I get to Where can I find		the … ?		
Go	upstairs downstairs	to the … floor.	Take	the lift. the stairs.
Take	the first the second	left. right.	It's	opposite the lifts. next to
It's	near along across at the end of	the corridor.		

12 Work with a partner. Practise this conversation.

A   Do you need/want any biros and pencils?
B   Yes, I need some biros and some pencils.
B   Yes, I need some pencils, but I don't need any biros.

Now partner A look at this page; partner B look at File 1 on page 158.

Ask partner B about two things on the equipment list.
What things does partner B need?

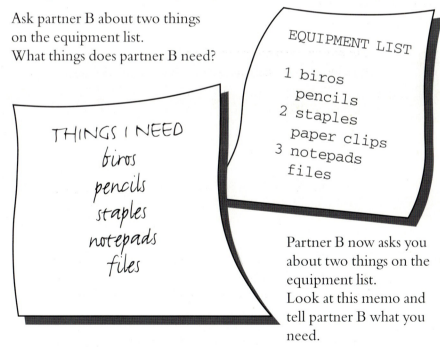

THINGS I NEED
biros
pencils
staples
notepads
files

EQUIPMENT LIST

1 biros
   pencils
2 staples
   paper clips
3 notepads
   files

Partner B now asks you about two things on the equipment list.
Look at this memo and tell partner B what you need.

Over to you

13 Work with a partner.
Draw a plan of your workplace. Mark on it some of the important places at work. Do not write their names! Prepare a short explanation for your partner.

Talking about your workplace

There are (3) floors in the building.
I work on the (ground) floor in the (mailroom).
I work in an office (on the second floor) with (two) other people.
My office is opposite / next to the lift / meeting room.
This is the (canteen). / These are the (lifts).

14 Work with a partner.
You are in your room at work. Your partner is a visitor.
Use your plan again. Give directions to different places while your partner follows them on the plan. See if your partner reaches the right place!

Look at page 19 to help you.

15 Work with a partner.
Partner A look at this page; partner B look at File 2 on page 158.

Here are nine people and their jobs. Read these sentences to partner B.
1 The marketing manager is next to the production manager.
2 The personnel manager is on the left.
3 The trainee is on the right of the assistant personnel manager.
4 The filing clerk is number nine.

Now listen to partner B's sentences. Who is on the left of the marketing manager?

Focus on grammar

A — Some, any *(Mengenbezeichnungen)*

	NICHT ZÄHLBAR	MEHRZAHL
STATEMENT	I want **some** coffee.	I need **some** staplers.
NEGATIVE	I don't want **any** coffee.	I don't need **any** staplers.
QUESTION	Is there **any** coffee left?	Do you need **any** staplers?

Wenn man die Antwort „Ja" auf eine Frage erwartet (höfliches Angebot oder Bitte), verwendet man **some**:
Would you like **some** coffee?
Can I have **some** staplers, please?

B — This/these, that/those

EINZAHL	**this**	**that**
MEHRZAHL	**these**	**those**

This/these *beziehen sich auf etwas, das sich in der Nähe des Sprechers befindet.*
– **This** is your office. – **This** desk is very large.
That/those *beziehen sich auf etwas, das weiter weg ist.*
– Check **that** drawer (over there).

C — Simple present (2) *(die einfache Gegenwart)*

STATEMENTS	QUESTIONS	NEGATIVES
I work	**do** I work?	I **don't** work
you work	**do** you work?	you **don't** work
we work	**do** we work?	we **don't** work
they work	**do** they work?	they **don't** work
he/she/it work**s**	**does** he/she/it work?	he/she/it **doesn't** work

SHORT ANSWERS
Yes, I/you/we/they **do**.   Yes, he/she/it **does**.
No, I/you/we/they **don't**.   No, he/she/it **doesn't**.

don't = do not
doesn't = does not

Merken Sie sich die Wortstellung bei Fragen mit Fragewörtern:
How do you travel to work?   **Who does** she help at work?
Where do they live?   **When does** he check the list?

3 An urgent order *Warm-up*

Office furniture and equipment

SYSTEM 7
Walton Well Street
Oxford OX2 7DX

Tel 01865 56768
Fax 01865 59234

Stahl Beckmann GmbH
Seebergstraße 12-18
44227 Dortmund

Germany

Date 8th October 19..

ORDER NO   6790 DS/am

Please supply the following goods:

CAT NO   6754 A
DETAILS   0,8mm steel
QTY   100 tons
UNIT PRICE   £186.40/ton
TOTAL   £18,640

1 Complete the sentences.

1 The order was from … to … .
2 It was for … .
3 The quantity was … .
4 The total value of the order was … .
5 The date of the order was … .

People at work

🎧 Emergency!

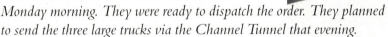

Dieter works in the purchasing department. He is responsible for materials and equipment from German suppliers. He orders these things, and he makes sure that deliveries arrive on time.

A few weeks ago, Dieter ordered some steel from a supplier in Dortmund, Stahl Beckmann. It was an urgent order and it was due by midday on Tuesday, 5th November. Stahl Beckmann called Dieter on Monday morning. They were ready to dispatch the order. They planned to send the three large trucks via the Channel Tunnel that evening.

The factory staff always listen to the radio at work. Dieter was in the factory with Jameel on Monday afternoon. When the four o'clock news started, they listened in shock …

"An hour ago, a fire started in the Channel Tunnel. French and British emergency teams are at the fire now. There are no casualties, but the Tunnel is shut – perhaps for several days."

"Quick!" Jameel said. "Book those trucks on a Calais–Dover ferry."
"This evening or tomorrow morning?" Dieter asked.
"It doesn't matter. Just try to get some places – any places! I expect thousands of people are on the phone to the ferry companies right now!"

Dieter phoned. He was lucky. There were still some places for them on the first ferry next morning – at six a.m. He booked them.
So the trucks crossed the Channel by ferry and arrived exactly on time. Jameel turned to Dieter and smiled. "You did a good job yesterday. Thanks!"

? Answer the questions.

1. What is Dieter's job at System 7 (UK)?
2. What is he responsible for?
3. When was the Stahl Beckmann order due in Oxford?
4. Was there a problem? Why?
5. How did the trucks cross the Channel?

People at work

3 Correct the sentences.

1. Dieter ordered the steel from a French supplier.
2. Dieter called the supplier on Monday morning.
3. Dieter and Jameel listened to the six o'clock news.
4. The Tunnel fire started at two o'clock on Monday afternoon.
5. The trucks crossed the Channel at six o'clock in the evening.
6. They arrived at System 7 late.

4 Complete the sentences with these words.

delivery • dispatch • due • ferry • on time • purchasing • supplier

1. Dieter is responsible for buying materials. He works in the … department.
2. Stahl Beckmann is a … to System 7 (UK).
3. The company planned to … the order by truck.
4. The order was … to arrive at midday.
5. The trucks travelled across the Channel by … .
6. The … arrived in Oxford at midday. The trucks were … .

5 Work with a partner. Complete the dialogues. Then practise them.

are (2x) • 's • was (3x) • were

DIETER IS TALKING TO MIKE PARKER AT THE END OF THE WEEK:
MIKE   How _are_¹ things in purchasing?
DIETER   Fine, thanks. It _'s_² a very interesting job.
MIKE   _Are_³ there any problems?
DIETER   Well, there _was_⁴ a big problem with an order the other day.
MIKE   What _was_⁵ that about?
DIETER   Three trucks of steel _were_⁶ on their way from Germany, and then there _was_⁷ a fire in the Channel Tunnel.

for • at • by (2x) • in (2x) • on (4x)

MIKE   Ah, yes! It was on the news. Tell me about it.
DIETER   Well, the supplier sent the order _by_⁸ truck _on_⁹ Monday morning.
MIKE   But then there was that fire _in_¹⁰ the Tunnel _in_¹¹ the afternoon.
DIETER   That's right. So we decided to bring the trucks over _by_¹² ferry.
MIKE   Was there any space _for_¹³ them?
DIETER   Yes, there was room _on_¹⁴ the first ferry _on_¹⁵ Tuesday morning.
MIKE   So the order wasn't late.
DIETER   No. The trucks arrived exactly _on_¹⁶ time _at_¹⁷ midday!

UNIT 3

6 Complete the sentences with the correct verb forms.

1. Dieter *didn't order* the steel from System 7. He … it from Stahl Beckman. (ordered / didn't order)
2. The supplier … Jameel. He … Dieter. (called / didn't call)
3. They … to the four o'clock news. They … to the one o'clock news. (listened / didn't listen)
4. The trucks … the Channel by ferry. They … via the Tunnel. (crossed / didn't cross)

7 Look at your sentences in Exercise 6. Form questions from them. Work with a partner. Ask and answer the questions.

Did Dieter order the steel from System 7?
No, he didn't.
Did Dieter order the steel from Stahl Beckman?
Yes, he did.

8 Form questions.

1. when (Dieter order) the steel
   When did Dieter order the steel?
2. what date (Stahl Beckmann dispatch) the order
3. how (the supplier dispatch) the steel
4. why (the trucks cross) by ferry
5. which ferry (the trucks use)
6. what time (the order arrive) at System 7 (UK)

9 Look at your questions in Exercise 8 again. Ask and answer them with a partner.

When did Dieter order the steel?
He ordered it on 8th October.

10 What are the infinitive forms of these verbs? (Look at page 129 to help you, if necessary.)

1. began – *to begin*   5. put
2. broke   6. ran
3. did   7. went
4. got   8. were

English at work

11 System 7 opened a sales office in Britain ten years ago. The office grew fast, and then production started, too.
That was six years ago. Two years ago the UK company also opened a small research and development (R&D) department. Today, the organization of the company looks like this.

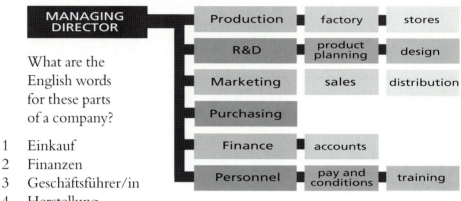

What are the English words for these parts of a company?

1 Einkauf
2 Finanzen
3 Geschäftsführer/in
4 Herstellung
5 Personalabteilung
6 Verkauf
7 Versand

12 Which departments do these three women work in? Use words from the organization chart.

I joined three years ago. I was a secretary in sales at that time. I did letters and reports, but I really liked working with figures. So I moved to finance. Now I work as Mr White's assistant. He's the senior accountant. I do the accounts every month.

I trained as an engineer. Then I worked at a large car maker for eight years. I was an assistant manager in a large design department. Then I joined System 7 two years ago. Here I am in charge of the new design team. It's only a small section, but it's mine. I really like that.

UNIT 3 26

I don't stay in the office much. I like to get out on the road, meet customers and get orders. I do that best. But I don't just think about selling the products in our catalogue. I also think about new products and new markets. That's an important part of a sales representative's job too.

13 Complete this news report. Use these verbs.
began • broke • broke down • broke out • crashed • did • got • put out • ran • were

A fire *broke out*[1] in the Channel Tunnel at 2 o'clock this afternoon. It seems that the Tunnel control system …[2]. Then two trains …[3]. The second one …[4] into the back of the first one. The fire …[5] because the crash …[6] the petrol tank of a truck on the first train. Emergency teams …[7] to the fire quickly, and they soon …[8] the fire. There …[9] no casualties, but the crash …[10] some damage to the Tunnel.

> **Time phrases** *(Adverbiale Bestimmungen der Zeit)*
> yesterday morning / evening   last week / month
> the day before yesterday   the night before last
> on Wednesday afternoon   two / a few days / years ago
>
> *Adverbiale Bestimmungen der Zeit können am Ende oder am Anfang des Satzes stehen.*

14 Make complete sentences.

1 Stahl Beckmann/on Monday morning/call
   Stahl Beckmann called on Monday morning.
2 Dieter/a few days ago/some steel/order
   A few days ago, Dieter ordered some steel
3 a fire/yesterday afternoon/in the Channel Tunnel/break out
4 the trucks/the Channel/on Tuesday morning/cross
5 Mike Parker/join/five years ago/System 7
6 System 7/a sales office in Britain/ten years ago/open

Over to you

15 Put the notes about Dieter in order. Work with a partner.

1 = G   2 = I

- A Did not like his first job and joined System 7's Hamburg branch;
- B Now works in purchasing in Oxford too;
- C Moved to System 7 in Munich nine months ago;
- D Joined System 7 (UK) two months ago;
- E Is responsible for supplies from Germany;
- F Left technical school and got a job at a supermarket;
- G Grew up in Hamburg with his parents and sister;
- H Worked in Munich as a trainee in purchasing;
- I Went to the local technical school and left at 16;

Indefinite article a/an

Dieter is **a** trainee. Mike is **an** assistant personnel manager.
Dieter ist Auszubildender *Mike ist Assistent in der Personalabteilung.*

*Bei Berufsbezeichnungen wird der unbestimmte Artikel **a/an** verwendet.*

Now tell your partner about Dieter. Start like this:
Dieter grew up in Hamburg with his parents and sister. He went to the local technical school until he was 16. Then he …

16 Now write notes about your life. Tell your partner about yourself. Use the expressions below.

at (age) • two years ago • last year • recently

17 Find out about your partner. Ask and answer questions.

Asking somebody questions

Questions about the past
When did you … ?
Where did you … ?
What did you … ?
How long did you … ?
Did you … ?

Questions about the present
When do you … ?
Where do you … ?
What do you … ?
How often do you … ?
Do you … ?

Focus on grammar

A Simple past: to be *(einfache Vergangenheit: to be)*

Statements	Questions	Negatives
I **was**	**was** I?	I **wasn't**
you **were**	**were** you?	you **weren't**
he/she/it **was**	**was** he/she/it?	he/she/it **wasn't**
we **were**	**were** we?	we **weren't**
they **were**	**were** they?	they **weren't**

Short answers
Yes, I/he/she/it **was**.   Yes, you/we/they **were**.
No, I/he/she/it **wasn't**. No, you/we/they **weren't**.

wasn't = was not
weren't = were not

> Merken Sie sich die Wortstellung bei Fragen mit Fragewörtern:
> **When was** it due?   **Where were** the trucks?   **Why were** they late?

B Simple past: regular verbs *(einfache Vergangenheit: regelmäßige Verben)*

Statements	Questions	Negatives
I work**ed**	**did** I work?	I **didn't** work
you call**ed**	**did** you call?	you **didn't** call
he/she/it look**ed**	**did** he/she/it look?	he/she/it **didn't** look
we talk**ed**	**did** we talk?	we **didn't** talk
they check**ed**	**did** they check?	they **didn't** check

Short answers
Yes, I/… **did**. *(für alle Personen gleich)*
No, I/… **didn't**. *(für alle Personen gleich)*

didn't = did not

> Merken Sie sich die Wortstellung bei Fragen mit Fragewörtern:
> **What did** he order?   **How did** they cross?   **When did** you arrive?

Das **simple past** bezieht sich auf eine abgeschlossene Handlung oder ein abgeschlossenes Geschehen in der Vergangenheit. Es wird oft bei Zeitbestimmungen wie **yesterday, last week, a year ago, in 1989** verwendet.

Achten Sie auf die Aussprache der Endungen:
[d] order**ed**, arriv**ed**; [t] book**ed**, talk**ed**; [ɪd] start**ed**.

plan → pla**nn**ed; stop → sto**pp**ed; travel → trave**ll**ed; supply → supp**lie**d
unregelmäßige Verben siehe Seite 129

4 Computers — Warm-up

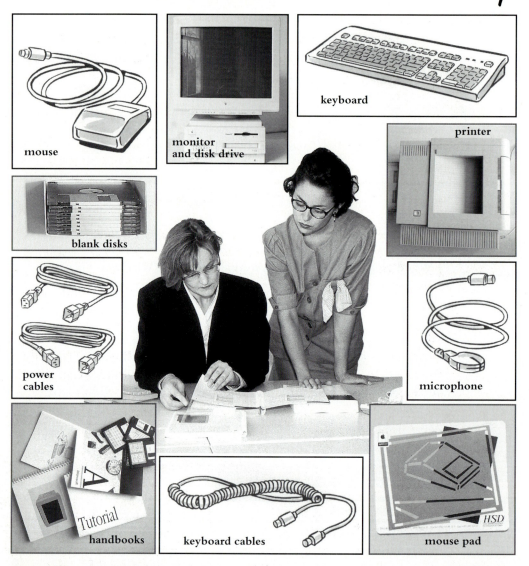

1 Petra has a new computer, but some parts are missing. Look at the photographs (the things she has) and the illustrations from the the user's handbook (the things she doesn't have). Make true sentences.

She has a monitor and a disk drive.
She doesn't have any power cables.

Work with a partner. Ask and answer questions.
Does she have a printer?   *Yes, she does.*
Does she have any power cables?   *No, she doesn't.*

People at work

🎧 Computer magic

Petra works with the marketing team at System 7. A few days ago her boss, Anna Wells, had an urgent phone call. It was Brian Tate, head of export sales.

"Anna, I really need your help," he said. "You know we have to fly to Munich this evening ..."

"Yes, you have to sell the new Home Office range to head office." Anna answered. "What's the problem?"

"They want our advertising leaflet – but in German. Can you do it by 5 p.m.?"

"What! It's 3.15 now! Why didn't you tell me about this weeks ago?"

"Anna, I'm really, really sorry. But could you help? Please! It's for their sales staff, so we only need 200 copies. We must have them this afternoon."

"Only 200! In German!" Anna laughed. "We can't do it." Then she looked across at Petra and said, "You may be lucky, this time, Brian. But don't do this to me again!"

Anna put the phone down, and explained the problem to Petra. Petra looked at the leaflet. "I can translate it and I can do the wordprocessing," she said. "But I may have a problem with the design. I'm not a designer!"

"Ah, but we needn't design it," Anna answered. "We can copy the English leaflet and keep the old design. Then we can just delete the English and key in your translation."

Petra made a new file and began to translate on-screen. It was sometimes difficult to make the German fit the spaces. But she was able to finish by 4.45.

She pressed Print and watched the leaflet print out. "There you are," she smiled at Anna. "Fantastic!" Anna said, and she set the printer for 200 copies.

"That's real computer magic – and some Petra magic too!"

HOME OFFICE

The latest in office furniture design from System 7 (UK) for use in the office and study at home.

The HOME OFFICE system offers the following special features:

People at work

2 Answer the questions.

1. Why did Brian Tate have to go to Munich?
2. What did he need for the German sales staff?
3. Why was Brian lucky?
4. What couldn't Petra do?
5. What did they do about this problem?

3 Complete the sentences with these words.

deleted • export sales • keyed in • printed out • translated • wordprocessing

1. System 7 sells in Britain. The company also gets … in other countries.
2. Petra learned … in Germany. She can do 60 words per minute.
3. Petra didn't need the English words and so she … them from the new file.
4. Petra … the English into German.
5. She sat at the wordprocessor and … the new text.
6. At the end, Anna … 200 copies of the leaflet.

4 Complete the dialogue. Then practise it.

a (4x) • *any* (2x) • *some* (3x) • *the* (5x)

ANNA WELLS IS ON THE PHONE TO THE OFFICE SERVICES DEPARTMENT:

RICK Hello. Office services.
ANNA Oh, hello, Rick. This is Anna Wells in …¹ marketing department.
RICK Ah, yes. We sent you …² PCII computer this morning. Are there …³ problems?
ANNA Well, yes. …⁴ things are missing. There aren't …⁵ power cables. And we don't have …⁶ keyboard or …⁷ mouse.
RICK Oh, sorry. Perhaps we didn't check …⁸ machine. You see, …⁹ people often take things from …¹⁰ new machines as spare parts for …¹¹ other computers.
ANNA Well, perhaps I could have …¹² "spare parts" from …¹³ new computer too!
RICK Sure. We can send you …¹⁴ missing items after lunch. Is that all right?
ANNA Fine. Thanks, Rick.

5 What are the infinitive forms of these verbs? (Look at page 129.)

1. had – *to have* 2. made 3. put 4. said 5. set 6. thought

6 Complete the sentences with the verbs from Exercise 5.

1 Where's the disk? I … it by the computer yesterday.
2 Hello! We … you were in New York!
3 "Anna, I'm really, really sorry," he … .
4 I … the fax machine to "Auto" and these faxes arrived last night.
5 Petra … no time to stop for coffee.
6 We … 20 copies of the report.

7 Complete the sentences.

can (2x) • *can't* (2x) • *could* • *couldn't* • *may* • *may not*

1 – … you speak German?
– Yes, and I … do wordprocessing as well.
2 The computer went dead, and I … understand why at first.
3 – … you help me, please? This computer handbook is in English.
– I … be able to help you, because I … speak English very well.
4 – … I have the day off tomorrow?
– No, I'm afraid you … . We're very busy at the moment.

could • *couldn't* • *must* • *mustn't* • *needn't* • *was able to* • *wasn't able to*

5 Petra … finish the German leaflet in time.
6 She … speak a little English when she was 14.
7 Lucy … finish the report because she was too busy.
8 Stahl Beckmann … send their trucks via the Channel Tunnel.
9 Brian … have the report by 5 p.m. The German sales reps need it.
10 Petra … go to the office on Sundays. It is the weekend.
11 You … smoke in restaurants in America. It is not allowed.

8 Complete the sentences with a correct modal verb.

1 Look! A bus is coming. *Can you see it? (können)*
2 Peter *couldn't* get up yesterday morning. He was ill. *(nicht können)*
3 Hello. Police? Quick! You … come quickly. *(müssen)*
4 Jane … do the report again. It's very good. *(nicht brauchen)*
5 Rob … swim when he was only three years old. *(können)*
6 Great! We've got some money, so we … go out for dinner *(können)* – and I … cook. *(nicht brauchen)*
7 Excuse me. I … carry these heavy bags by myself. *(nicht können)* … you help me, please? *(können)*

English at work

9 The picture at the top shows the marketing office early this morning. The picture at the bottom shows the office now, at 5 p.m. Compare it with the first picture and find the differences.

clean/dirty • down/up • empty/full • labelled/unlabelled • off/on • open/shut • tidy/untidy

*Anna's desk lamp was off before, but it's on now.
Anna's desk lamp is on now, but it was off this morning.*

10 Work with a partner. Study the keyboard and the file menu. Then complete the answers to the trainee's questions.

A How can I make a space between words?
B *Click onto the right place with the mouse and press the space bar.*
A I want to delete this word. What do I have to do?
B Click onto the word and press …¹ delete
A I want to start a fresh line. What do I do?
B At the end of the line press …² return
A I'd like to stop for a cup of coffee. How can I make sure I don't lose my work?
B Click onto the file menu and select …³ save = Speichern
A I need to key in the next line in capital letters. How do I do that?
B Press …⁴ shift and key in the line.
A How can I go up one line and one word to the right?
B Click onto the right place or press the …⁵ cursor keys.
A That's all the text. Now I need to print a copy. What do I have to do?
B Click onto the file menu and select …⁶ print.
A Now I want to close the file and go to lunch. What should I do?
B Click onto the file menu and select …⁷ close
A Thanks very much! That was a big help!

Now practise the dialogue with your partner.

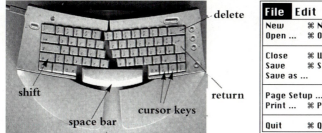 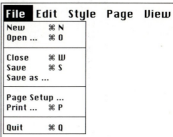

11 Complete these sentences with the correct English words.

Petra took the *(Diskette)* …¹ with the English leaflet on it and put it into the *(Diskettenlaufwerk)* …². Then she made a *(Kopie)* …³ of the file. She *(löschte)* …⁴ the English text and started to translate *(am Bildschirm)* …⁵. She *(gab ein)* …⁶ the German using the *(Tastatur)* …⁷. When she was ready she *(klickte … an)* …⁸ the file menu with the mouse and selected *(Speichern)* …⁹. Then she *(druckte aus)* …¹⁰ the new leaflet on the *(Drucker)* …¹¹.

Over to you

12 Work with a partner.
Find the English for these phrases in "Computer magic" (page 31).

1. Ich brauche unbedingt deine Hilfe.
2. Was ist das Problem?
3. Schaffst du das bis 17 Uhr?
4. Wir müssen sie heute Nachmittag haben.
5. Vielleicht hast du diesmal Glück.
6. Wir brauchen es nicht gestalten.
7. Dann können wir das Englische einfach löschen.

13 Your company plans to open an office in the United Kingdom. Your boss wants to buy the office furniture there.

Translate this brochure about a computer workstation *(Arbeitsplatz)* for her.

Computer Workstation

Only **£139**

This computer workstation has everything that your computer staff need. There is a shelf for the monitor above a large desk. Below is a sliding shelf for the keyboard, with another for the mouse-pad. Under this is another sliding shelf for the printer. The computer workstation is available in two colours: grey and black.

Size: 770H x 590W x 510D mm

Code   Description   Price
303-300   Computer workstation – grey   £139
303-400   Computer workstation – black   £139

UNIT 4   36

Focus on grammar

A

Can/could

FÄHIGKEIT
I **can** type. *(Ich kann tippen)*
I **could** type when I was 15.
(Ich konnte tippen, als ich 15 war.)

MÖGLICHKEIT
I **can** finish the report today.
I **was able to** finish the report yesterday.
(Ich habe es geschafft, ...)

HÖFLICHE BITTE
Can/Could you tell me the time?
Can I help you?

ERLAUBNIS
Can I go to the cinema this evening?
(Darf ich heute Abend ins Kino gehen?)

Can't/couldn't

I **can't** type. *(Ich kann nicht tippen)*
I **couldn't** type when I was 15.
(Ich konnte nicht tippen, als ich 15 war.)

I **can't** finish the report. I'm busy.
I **wasn't able to/couldn't** finish the report yesterday.
(Ich habe es nicht geschafft, ...)

No, you **can't** go.
(Nein, du darfst nicht gehen.)

B

Must

GESETZ
You **must** drive on the left in England.
(In England müssen Sie links fahren.)

NOTWENDIGKEIT
We **must** have the report by 5 p.m.
(Wir müssen den Bericht bis 17 Uhr haben.)

Mustn't

You **mustn't** smoke here.
(Sie dürfen hier nicht rauchen.)

We **mustn't** lose this contract.
(Wir dürfen diesen Vertrag nicht verlieren.)

C

Needn't

We **needn't** design it.
(Wir müssen/brauchen es nicht gestalten.)

D

May

MÖGLICHKEIT
You **may** be lucky.
(Vielleicht haben Sie Glück.)

ERLAUBNIS
May I have a piece of cake, please?
(Darf ich bitte ein Stück Kuchen haben?)

May not

I **may not** be able to finish it.
(Es ist möglich, dass ich es nicht schaffe.)

5   A visitor — Warm-up

1 Complete the sentences.

1. Miss Ellis came at … to see … .
2. Mike Parker had an appointment at … with … .
3. The man in reception at 9.15 was … .
4. He had an appointment to see … at … .
5. They wanted to discuss … .
6. … could not see Mr Macgregor at 9.15 because he was in a … .

People at work

A visitor for Mr Patel

The receptionist, Jean Glass, was at work as usual this morning.

RECEPTIONIST Good morning. Can I help you?
MACGREGOR Hello. I have an appointment with Mr Patel at 10 o'clock. But I'm afraid I'm early. The name is Macgregor.
RECEPTIONIST Ah, yes. I'll just phone Mr Patel's office. He may be free now. (On the phone) Could I speak to Mr Patel, please?
DIETER I'm afraid he's in a meeting at the moment. It won't finish before 9.45.
RECEPTIONIST Well, Mr Macgregor is here to see him.
DIETER All right. I'll show him round the factory.
RECEPTIONIST Fine. I'll send him to you … Petra. Can I ask a favour?
PETRA Sure. What can I do for you?
RECEPTIONIST Could you take Mr Macgregor to Dieter's office? He has an appointment with Jameel, but he's in a meeting at the moment.

PETRA Yes, of course. Please come this way, Mr Macgregor.
MACGREGOR Thank you.
PETRA Not at all. Is your firm local, Mr Macgregor?
MACGREGOR No. I'm here from Glasgow.
PETRA Did you have a good journey?
MACGREGOR Yes, thanks, but I got to Oxford at 7.00. That's why I'm early.
PETRA How did you come to Oxford?
MACGREGOR I came down by train.

PETRA Well, here we are. (Petra opens the door) Dieter, here's Mr Macgregor. Mr Macgregor, this is Dieter Salter.
DIETER How do you do?
MACGREGOR Pleased to meet you. And thank you again, Miss Hoffmann.
PETRA You're very welcome. Goodbye.
DIETER Well, first, Mr Macgregor, how about a cup of coffee before I show you round the factory?
MACGREGOR I'd love a cup.
DIETER Would you like milk and sugar?
MACGREGOR Sugar, but no milk, please.
DIETER Here you are.
MACGREGOR Thanks very much. … This tastes very good!

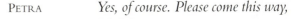

People at work

2 Answer the questions.

1. Who works in reception?
2. What happened at 9.15?
3. Who answered the phone in Jameel Patel's office?
4. Where was Jameel Patel?
5. Who took the visitor to Dieter's office?
6. What did Dieter give the visitor?
7. What do you think happened after that?

3 Match the expressions (1–8) to their meanings (A–H).

1 = C

1	at the moment	A	I want to help you. Tell me what to do.
2	Can I ask a favour?	B	I'm sorry to say that
3	You're very welcome.	C	now
4	how about	D	Could you do something for me?
5	How can I help you?	E	I suggest
6	I'm afraid	F	do you want
7	What can I do for you?	G	I was happy to help you.
8	would you like	H	I want to help you. Tell me what to do.

4 Complete the sentences. Choose from these expressions.

by bicycle • by car • by ferry • by plane • by ship • by train • by truck
by air • by rail • by road • by sea

1. Mr Macgregor came to Oxford *by train*.
2. Petra and Dieter came to Britain ... .
3. Mike took them from their hotel to the office ... .
4. Stahl Beckmann sent System 7's order ... .
5. It crossed the Channel ... .

5 Work with a partner. Complete the dialogues. Then practise them.

'd • 'll (3x) • will (2x) • won't • would (3x)

VISITOR   Excuse me, I have an appointment with Mr Black.
RECEPTIONIST I...¹ just check that for you. Yes, at 10 o'clock. I...² call Mr Black's office. What name is it, please.
VISITOR   Robert Stevens.

VISITOR   I have an appointment with Mr West at 11 o'clock. I'm a little early.

RECEPTIONIST   I'm afraid Mr West is in a meeting at the moment. It …³ finish until 10.45. …⁴ you like to take a seat? I…⁵ call his office and someone …⁶ come and show you round.

SECRETARY   Mr West …⁷ be free in ten minutes. …⁸ you like a cup of coffee before he comes?

VISITOR   Thank you, I…⁹ love one.

SECRETARY   …¹⁰ you like milk and sugar?

VISITOR   Just milk, please.

could (3x) • *didn't* (2x) • *had* • *is* (3x) • *'m* (2x)

CALLER   Hello. This …¹¹ Boris Bronowski of Moscow Office Systems. …¹² I speak to Mrs Lawrence, please?

RECEPTIONIST   I…¹³ sorry. I …¹⁴ hear that. …¹⁵ you repeat that, please? This line …¹⁶ bad.

CALLER   …¹⁷ I speak to Mrs Lawrence, please?

RECEPTIONIST   Mrs Lawrence …¹⁸ away on maternity leave.

CALLER   I…¹⁹ afraid I …²⁰ understand that. Away on what?

RECEPTIONIST   Maternity leave. She …²¹ a baby last week.

CALLER   Ah! Great news! Please give her my best wishes.

6   Write object questions.

1   who (you meet) last night
    Who did you meet last night?
2   who (you interview) on Thursday afternoon
3   who (the trainees take) to the hotel
4   who (Dieter show) round the factory

Now change the questions into subject questions.
Who met you last night?

7   Write questions with *what*.

1   what (happen) at the meeting yesterday
    What happened at the meeting yesterday?
2   what (she do) this morning at work
    What did she do this morning at work?
3   what (come) in the mail this morning
4   what (Mr Macgregor say) to the receptionist
5   what (happen) after coffee
6   what (Dieter show) Mr Macgregor

English at work

8 Work with a partner.
Find the English for these phrases in "A visitor for Mr Patel" (page 39).

1 Guten Morgen. Kann ich Ihnen helfen?
2 Ich habe einen Termin um 10 Uhr mit Mr Patel.
3 Könnte ich bitte Mr Patel sprechen?
4 Es tut mir leid, er ist momentan in einer Besprechung.
5 Bitte folgen Sie mir, Mr Macgregor.
6 Hatten Sie eine angenehme Reise?
7 Und nochmals vielen Dank, Miss Hoffmann.
8 Möchten Sie eine Tasse Kaffee?

9 Work with a partner. Complete these conversations.

afternoon • appointment • come • phone • seat

VISITOR Good …[1]. I have an …[2] with Mr Parker at 3 o'clock.
RECEPTIONIST Would you like to take a …[3]? I'll just …[4] his office and someone will …[5] and meet you.

come • early • finish • free • have • here • meeting • name • speak

MR WEST Good morning. My …[6] is West. I …[7] an appointment with Mr Brown. I'm a bit …[8].
RECEPTIONIST I'll just phone his office. He may be …[9] now.
(ON THE PHONE)
Could I …[10] to Mr Brown, please?
SECRETARY I'm afraid he's in a …[11] at the moment. It won't …[12] before 10.45.
RECEPTIONIST Well, Mr West is …[13] to see him.
SECRETARY All right. I'll …[14] and meet him.

by • firm • from • journey • thanks • to

SECRETARY Is your …[15] local Mr West?
MR WEST No, I'm here …[16] Manchester.
SECRETARY Did you have a good …[17]?
MR WEST Yes, …[18], but I got here very early.
SECRETARY How did you come …[19] London?
MR WEST I came down …[20] car.

about • before • like • love • no • office •
take • welcome • you • you're

SECRETARY	This is Mr Brown's …²¹. Please …²² a seat.
MR WEST	Thank you.
SECRETARY	How …²³ a cup of coffee …²⁴ Mr Brown comes?
MR WEST	I'd …²⁵ a cup.
SECRETARY	Would you …²⁶ milk and sugar?
MR WEST	Just milk, …²⁷ sugar, thanks.
SECRETARY	Here …²⁸ are.
MR WEST	Thank you very much.
SECRETARY	…²⁹ very …³⁰.

Now practise these conversations with your partner.

10 On their way round the company Mr Macgregor asked Dieter questions about System 7.
Give Dieter's answers. (Look back at Units 1-4 if necessary.)

MACGREGOR	How many people work in manufacturing?
DIETER	*About 200 people work in the factory.*
MACGREGOR	Do you work in manufacturing too?
DIETER	No, I don't. I work in …¹.
MACGREGOR	What do you do in purchasing?
DIETER	I'm responsible for …².
MACGREGOR	Is this place System 7's head office?
DIETER	No. Our head office is in …³.
MACGREGOR	Does System 7 have operations anywhere else?
DIETER	Yes, we have …⁴.
MACGREGOR	When did System 7 start in Britain?
DIETER	We started in Britain …⁵.
MACGREGOR	Did the company start in the UK with a factory or a sales office – or both?
DIETER	It started …⁶.

Now practise the conversation with a partner.

Over to you

Looking after visitors

Good morning/afternoon. Can I help you?

I'll just phone (Mr Patel's) office. He may be free now. What name is it, please?

I'm afraid (Mr Patel) is in a meeting just now. Would you like to take a seat for a moment?

(Mr Patel) is busy at the moment. Someone will come to meet you.

(Mr Patel) will be free in ten minutes. Would you like some tea/coffee before he comes?

Would you like milk and sugar?

Would you like me to show you round while (Mr Patel) is busy?
Did you have a good journey to (Oxford)?
How did you travel/come to (Oxford)?

---

11 Work with a partner.
Partner A look at this page; partner B look at File 3 on page 159.

Act these conversations. Make notes to help you first, if necessary.

1 Partner A is a receptionist; partner B is a visitor. Partner A begins:

- Sagen Sie Guten Morgen. Fragen Sie den Besucher, ob Sie ihm helfen können.
- Bitten Sie den Besucher, einen Moment Platz zu nehmen. Sie werden im Büro von Mrs Reece anrufen: Mrs Reece wird ihn abholen kommen.

2 Partner A is a visitor; partner B is Petra Hoffmann. Partner B begins:

- Sie stellen sich vor: Sie heißen Brooks und kommen aus Liverpool.
- Sie sagen: Mit dem Zug.
- Sie nehmen das Angebot gerne an.
- Sie möchten nur Zucker, keine Milch.
- Sie bedanken sich.

UNIT 5

Focus on grammar

A The future: will *(das Futur: will)*

STATEMENTS	QUESTIONS	NEGATIVES
I**'ll work**	**will** I **work**?	I **won't work**
you**'ll work**	**will** you **work**?	you **won't work**
he/she/it**'ll work**	**will** he/she/it **work**?	he/she/it **won't work**
we**'ll work**	**will** we **work**?	we **won't work**
they**'ll work**	**will** they **work**?	they **won't work**

SHORT ANSWERS
Yes, I/… **will**. *(Für alle Personen gleich)*
No, I/… **won't**. *(Für alle Personen gleich)*

> 'll = will
> won't = will not

> **Will** *wird für Voraussagen über zukünftige Ereignisse benutzt, auf die wir keinen Einfluss haben.*
> It **won't finish** before 9.45.
> **Will** *wird auch für spontane Entscheidungen, Angebote und Versprechungen verwendet.*
> All right. I**'ll** show him round the factory.

B Would

Would you like some coffee?
I'd like/love a cup.

> 'd = would

Would you like … ? *wird für ein höfliches Angebot oder für eine Einladung verwendet.* **Would** *kann auch nach* **love**, **recommend**, **suggest** *und* **prefer** *verwendet werden.*

C Subject and object questions with who and what

Who called Jean? (who = subject)   **Who did** Jean call? (who = object)

What hit the car? (what = subject)   **What did** the car hit? (what = object)

> *Merken Sie sich: Die Wortstellung bei Fragen mit* **who** *oder* **what** *als Subjekt ist die gleiche wie in einem Aussagesatz.*
> **Who** called Jean?   **Peter** called Jean.

Test 1

1 Match the details (1–5) with the following items (A–E).
A Company position 1 Smith
B First name 2 Susan
C Date of birth 3 Marketing trainee
D Address 4 15/11/78
E Family name 5 75 High Street, Stanford, Oxon SN7 8NQ

2 Write out these dates.
1 03/01 - *3rd January* 3 02/12 5 23/03
2 15/05 4 21/02 6 06/09

3 Complete the sentences with the correct names of departments.
1 The ... department buys materials and equipment from suppliers.
2 The ... department makes goods for the company to sell.
3 The ... department looks after the company's money.
4 The ... department deals with pay and conditions of the staff.

4 Complete the conversations. Use the following words:
along • at • in • of • on • opposite • to (2x)
A Excuse me. How do I get ...¹ Susan Fenton's office, please?
B She's ...² Room 123 ...³ the ground floor, so go ...⁴ this corridor, and take a lift ...⁵ the ground floor. Her room is ...⁶ the end ...⁷ the corridor, ...⁸ the canteen.

5 Put the verbs in the correct forms of the *simple present*.
1 Petra and Dieter ... German at work in Oxford. They ... English. (speak)
2 Mike Parker ... in Germany. He ... in Britain. (live)
3 Dieter: "I ... in the marketing department. I ... in purchasing." (work)
4 Petra: "Dieter and I ... Britain – it's great! But Dieter sometimes ... the food in the company canteen!" (like)

6 Form questions and answers. Use the *simple past*.
A from Munich? / When / you arrive – *When did you arrive from Munich?*
B We / yesterday / arrive – *We arrived yesterday.*
A you travel / to Oxford? / How
B We travel / by bus. / there
A to the hotel? / you get / What time
B at 9.45 / We get / in the evening. / there

7 Translate these expressions into English.
1 Entschuldigen Sie. Sind Sie die neuen Auszubildenden aus München?
2 Es freut mich, Sie kennen zu lernen. Ich heiße Petra Hoffmann.
3 Hallo! Schön, Sie wiederzusehen. Wie geht es Ihnen?
4 Mir geht's gut, danke. Und Ihnen?

Test 2

1 Give the English for the following:
1. löschen – *delete*
2. Laufwerk
3. Tastatur
4. Bildschirm
5. Maus
6. Drucker
7. ausdrucken
8. speichern

2 Complete the sentences.
1. The lights are on. They should be *off*.
2. The windows are dirty. They should be ... .
3. The coffee machine is empty. It should be ... .
4. The desk drawers are open. They should be ...
5. The window blinds are down. They should be ... .

3 Complete the sentences to show how people / things travel.
1. In Britain, goods usually travel (🚚) *by road*, and not (🚃) *by rail*.
2. You can use the Tunnel to travel between Britain and France. You can also go (✈) ... or (🚢) ... .
3. Helen goes to work (🚗) ... , Tony goes (🏍) ... , and Robin usually goes (🚌) ... .

4 Complete the sentences with correct modal verbs.
1. I looked in all the drawers, but I ... find my keys. *(nicht können)*
2. Quick! We ... miss the train! *(nicht dürfen)*
3. We ... finish the job today *(nicht brauchen)*, but we ... finish it tomorrow. *(müssen)*
4. A ... I see the manager, please? *(dürfen)*
   B I'm sorry, but you ... see him now. He's in a meeting. *(nicht dürfen)*

5 Make questions. Put the verbs in the *simple past*.
1. what / see / he – *What did he see?*
2. call / who / him – *Who called him?*
3. they / think / what
4. she / who / phone
5. do / what / we
6. to him / happen / what

6 Translate these expressions into English.
1. Könnten Sie mir helfen, bitte?
2. Guten Tag. Kann ich Ihnen helfen?
3. Es tut mir leid, aber sie ist momentan in einer Besprechung.
4. Hatten Sie eine angenehme Reise von London?
5. Möchten Sie eine Tasse Kaffee?
6. Ich hätte gern eine Tasse Tee.

6 Changing jobs — Warm-up

1 Do you remember? Match the people to their job titles (A–F).

A the production manager
B the marketing manager
C a receptionist
D the personnel manager
E the assistant personnel manager
F the export sales manager

2 Do you remember?

1 Who welcomed Petra and Dieter to System 7 (UK)?
   Mike Parker did. He's the assistant personnel manager.
2 Who told Dieter to book a ferry for the trucks from Germany?
3 Who showed Petra her new office?
4 Who showed Petra how her computer worked?
5 Who asked Anna Wells to translate the sales leaflet?
6 Who asked Mr Macgregor: "Can I help you?"
7 Who showed Mr Macgregor to Dieter's office?

People at work

Back to personnel again

LUCY   Good afternoon, Petra and Dieter. Thanks for coming. So … You started last October, and now it's January. How do you like it?

PETRA   It's very good.

DIETER   But we don't like your English winter! It's not a real winter at all!

LUCY   True. Well, I can't change the weather, but I can change your jobs. I'd like to talk about that now.

PETRA   But I'm still a beginner in marketing.

DIETER   And I feel the same in purchasing.

LUCY   Well, the reports about you are very good. Have a look at them.

MEMO

To: Lucy Reece
From: Anna Wells
Subject: Petra Hoffmann
Date: 10th January

Here are the notes about Petra which you wanted. She came to marketing three months ago and she is a great help. She is good at office work and she works well with the others. We are very sorry she is going. One thing: I think Petra should have some contact with customers. Perhaps she should work in sales.

MEMO

To: L Reece
From: J Patel
Subject: D Salter
Date: 11th January

You asked for a quick memo about Dieter. He is a fast learner and a hard-working, intelligent member of the team. His German is very useful with our German customers. I am sorry that he must change jobs, but I am sure he will do well. One thing: I think he should stay in the field of supplies and transport. Could he work in distribution?

PETRA   Wow! This is really nice!

DIETER   Yes, this one is too.

LUCY   So we think you're ready for a change. You should get some experience of other jobs. Petra, we want to put you in export sales with Brian Tate.

PETRA   Oh. Brian Tate … We did a quick job for him for the Munich sales conference.

LUCY   Yes, Anna wasn't very happy about that! But don't worry. Brian can teach you a lot. Now, Dieter, we want to move you to export distribution. That's Paul Duval's section.

DIETER   Great. Paul and I get on well.

LUCY   Fine. Well, I hope you two enjoy your new jobs.

DIETER   When do we start?

LUCY   Probably next Monday. But go and ask your new bosses about that.

People at work

3 Answer the questions.

1. What does Lucy Reece say they are ready for?
2. Where does Anna Wells think Petra should work? Why?
3. Where does Jameel Patel think Dieter should work? Why?
4. Where does Lucy actually put them?

4 Complete the sentences with these words.

customers • distribution • experience • memos • purchasing • sales conference

1. At the moment, Dieter works in … .
2. Jameel and Anna wrote short … to Lucy about Dieter and Petra.
3. Petra works in the marketing office, and so she does not meet any … .
4. Anna knows all about computers. She has ten years' … of working with them.
5. System 7 has its own trucks for … to customers all over the UK.
6. Brian Tate went to a … in Munich.

5 Match the expressions (1–6) to their meanings (A–F).

1 = E

1. beginner
2. do well
3. get on well
4. Good afternoon.
5. How do you like it?
6. One thing:

A. like each other, enjoy being together
B. be successful
C. Hello. (after midday)
D. There is one special thing to think about:
E. person with little or no experience
F. What do you think of it?

6 Work with a partner. Complete the dialogues. Then practise them.

are • is • 'm (2x) • 's • was (2x) • were

PETRA MEETS BRIAN IN THE CANTEEN:

PETRA Excuse me, Brian. …¹ you free for a minute? It…² about my new job with you.

BRIAN Ah, yes, hello, Petra. I…³ very pleased that Lucy is sending you to us. I need some help at the moment, because my assistant Lizzie Lawrence …⁴ on maternity leave. And thank you for the leaflets, by the way. They …⁵ a great help, too.

PETRA How …⁶ the sales conference?

BRIAN It …⁷ very successful, thanks to your translation.

PETRA Oh, I…⁸ pleased about that!

UNIT 6

can • can't • must • mustn't • needn't

BRIAN When …⁹ you start?
PETRA I'm afraid I …¹⁰ start this week. I …¹¹ help Anna for a few days.
BRIAN Well, you …¹² start before Monday, but you …¹³ let me wait for you too long!

'll • will • won't

PETRA …¹⁴ I deal with customers in my new job?
BRIAN Well, you …¹⁵ deal with them all the time, but you …¹⁶ certainly be busy all the time!

7 Complete the sentences.

Expressions with 'have'

have a bath / a shower / a wash
have a sleep / a rest / a day off / a holiday / a game of (football)
have a drink / a snack / a meal
have tea / coffee / breakfast / lunch / dinner / supper
have a look for (something) / a look at (something)

1 Your face is dirty. You should … .
2 I'm thirsty. Let's go to the bar and … .
3 I feel ill. Could I … work today, please?
4 Come and … this! I think it's real gold!
5 Aunt Clare often gets tired, so she usually … in the afternoon.
6 Tony doesn't get hungry in the middle of the day, so he doesn't usually … .

8 Complete the sentences with *should* or *shouldn't*.

1 – I feel ill this morning.
  – You *should* stay in bed. You … go to work.
2 – I just can't get on with our new boss. He's always angry with me.
  – You … accept that. You … tell the personnel manager.
3 – That new photocopier breaks down all the time. I'd like to hit it!
  – Well, you certainly … do that! You … ask someone to repair it.
4 – This job advert in the newspaper looks good, so I'm writing this application letter.
  – Fine, but you … write it again. You … send one without spelling mistakes. Another thing: you … forget to write the date.

English at work

9 Dieter wants to set up a fax for his new office in export distribution. Match the instructions (1–6) to the cartoons (A–F). Add the verbs.

disconnect • do not cover • do not put (2x) • keep (2x)

(1 = E) Disconnect the fax in case of lightning.

1 … the fax in case of lightning.
2 … enough space (10 cm) between the fax and other objects.
3 … the fax away from heaters and air cooling systems.
4 … the fax at any time.
5 … objects on top of the fax.
6 … the fax's electrical cords *(Stromkabel)* where people walk.

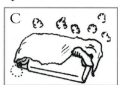

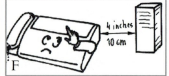

10 Petra wants to know about System 7 (UK)'s sales in Britain and other markets. Study the pie charts and complete the explanations.

three quarters • two thirds • half • a third • a quarter • an eighth

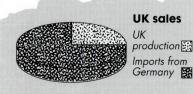

CHART I
1 *Three quarters of UK sales comes from imports from Germany.*
2 … of UK sales comes from UK …

CHART II
3 … of UK production sells in the UK.
4 … of … production sells abroad.

CHART III
5 … of UK exports sells in Germany.
6 … of UK … sells in France.
7 … of … sells in … .
8 … of …

11 Petra wants to know about System 7 (UK)'s exports and imports in recent years.

Work with a partner. Study the graphs and make sentences.
Use the table "Talking about sales figures" below to help you.

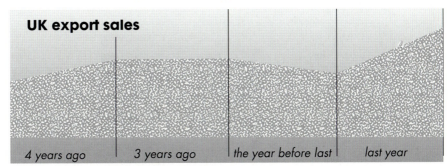

GRAPH 1

1. *Export sales rose slowly four years ago.*
2. Exports remained … three years ago.
3. … fell … two … ago.
4. Export … rose … a year … .

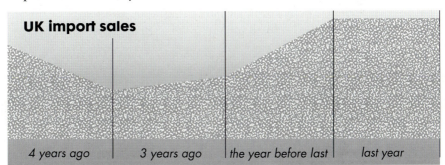

GRAPH 2

5. Import sales … rapidly … years ago.
6. Imports … slowly …
7. … sales … the year …
8. … remained …

Talking about sales figures

Exports	rose	rapidly	four years ago.
Export sales	fell	slowly	three years ago.
Imports		remained constant	two years ago. / the year before last.
Import sales			a year ago. / last year.

53 UNIT 6

Over to you

12 Karen and Andy are both 17. They left school last year, and now they are at college. They are on a course called Basic Skills for Business. They like the course because it is flexible. Everybody does office administration, book-keeping and word processing. Then there are special courses such as languages, computer studies and economics.

KAREN:
"I like this course. It's really useful. It gives you the basics, so you can go out and get a job in any kind of company, but there are extras like languages. That means you can be flexible. I'm not very good at working with figures and book-keeping and so I don't want to work in finance.
I'm good at languages, and on this course I can do French and German. For me that's really important. I want to get a job with an international company and use my languages."

ANDY:
"I'm very different from Karen, but the course is good for me too. I'm not very good at languages, so I don't do them. They say I'm stupid, and everybody needs languages now, but I'm just not interested. For me, computer skills are the big thing. I'm on the computer studies course, and I really like that. And I'm pretty good at computer programming now. I quite like office administration. Everybody needs to know about that. But I want to be a computer specialist one day."

She's	good at	book-keeping.
He's	not very good at	computer programming.
I'm		languages.
You're		office administration.
		telephone work.
		wordprocessing.
		working with figures.
		working with people.
		…

UNIT 6

She He	wants to doesn't want to should/shouldn't may/may not	be become	a an	accountant. clerical worker. computer programmer. manager. receptionist.
I You	want to don't want to should/shouldn't may/may not			salesperson. secretary. …

Work with a partner. Make sentences about Karen and Andy.
Start like this:
Karen is good at …
She isn't very good at …
She doesn't want to be a/an …
She may become a/an …

Now talk about yourself. Make more sentences. Start like this:
I'm good at …
I'm not very good at …
I don't want to be a/an …
I may become a/an …

Now ask your partner questions like these:
What are you good at?
What aren't you very good at?
What do you want to be?

Do you agree with your partner? Make sentences like these:
I agree. I think you should be a/an … .
I don't agree. You shouldn't be … . I think you should be … .

Should/should not

Verpflichtung
You **should** get some experience of other jobs.
(Sie sollten Erfahrungen in anderen Positionen sammeln.)
He **shouldn't** ask her to do it. *(Er sollte sie nicht bitten, es zu tun.)*

Empfehlung
You look ill. I think you **should** go to a doctor.
(Sie sehen krank aus. Sie sollten zum Arzt gehen.)

7   An order — Warm-up

1 You and a partner have a flat and you would like to buy the following:

a dishwasher • a telephone • a TV • a video recorder • a washing machine

But you can only afford three of these things.
Which three do you choose? Why?

2 Do a class survey.
Which are the top three choices? Is one of them a telephone?
Why?/Why not?

People at work

A phone call from Sweden

Petra was alone in the office on her third day with export sales. There was a lot to do. Here is one of her phone calls.

"Good morning. Export sales. How can I help you?"
"Could I speak to Mr Tate or Mrs Lawrence, please?"
"I'm sorry, but Mr Tate is visiting customers in Holland this week. And I'm doing Mrs Lawrence's job now. Can I help?"
"Please. It's very urgent."
"What's the problem?" she asked.
"Perhaps you can help me. I'm Olof Vennberg of Larsen Distribution."
"Could you spell that, please, Mr …" Petra reached for a pen.
"Vennberg. That's V…e…double-n…b…e…r…g."
"Was that G for Golf?"
"That's right. … Now, Mr Tate quoted for some office furniture in November. We accepted a lower quote from another supplier. But now they're bankrupt. They can't supply!"
"That's terrible!" Petra said.
"Yes. So please can you help? I need the order in a week."
"I'll try. What number is it? I'll check our stock lists and call you back."
"Thanks. It's 5633-BT77."
"Right. Goodbye for now, Mr Vennberg."

Petra found the Larsen quote and then she checked the stock lists on the computer. There were problems. For example, they were 80 desks short.

160 grey 3-drawer desks (304-503)
135 grey 6-drawer desks (304-523)
365 grey medium-back chairs (305-451)

UK STOCK LIST		
REF	DESCRIPTION	QTY
304-500	Desk, 3-drawer, black	238
304-503	Desk, 3-drawer, grey	80
304-520	Desk, 6-drawer, black	471
304-523	Desk, 6-drawer, grey	189
305-450	Chair, medium-back, red	316
305-451	Chair, medium-back, grey	247

Then Petra had an idea. She called up the export sales file. She was right. It showed a large export order to System 7 in Munich. "They can probably supply," she thought. She telephoned Brian Tate in Amsterdam and head office in Munich. They both agreed. Finally, she called Olof Vennberg back.

"Hello, it's Petra Hoffmann here. I've got good news for you, Mr Vennberg."
"Wonderful!" he shouted back. "Miss Hoffmann, I promise you Larsen Distribution will never use a different supplier again!"

People at work

3 Answer the questions.

1. What section is Petra now in?
2. How does Olof Vennberg know Brian Tate?
3. What is the problem with the other supplier?
4. How soon does Olof Vennberg need the order from System 7?
5. Look at Petra's notes and the UK stock list. What other problem does she find?
6. How can System 7 supply the full order?

4 Complete the sentences with these words.

bankrupt • quoted • reference • urgent • valid

1. Please finish this report as soon as possible. It's very … .
2. Brian Tate … Olof Vennberg a price of £37,000.
3. The company has gone out of business. It's … .
4. I can't find the file because I don't know the … number.
5. My new passport is … for ten years. What about yours?

5 Work with a partner. Ask and answer questions about Brian Tate.

1. (9.45) Is Mr Tate visiting the factory with Mr Honda just now?
   No, he isn't visiting the factory with Mr Honda just now. He's calling the agency in Spain.
2. (10.20) Is Mr Tate visiting the factory with Mr Honda at the moment?
3. (10.50) Is Mr Tate calling the agency in Spain right now?
4. (12.15) Is Mr Tate finishing the sales report just now?
5. (1.45) Is Mr Tate preparing for the sales conference at the moment?
6. (3.00) Is Mr Tate preparing for the sales conference right now?

DIARY

- 9.30–10.30 ~~Visit the factory with Mr Honda~~
- 9.30–10.00 Call the agency in Spain
- 10.45–11.15 ~~Call the agency in Spain~~
- 10.15–11.45 Prepare for the sales conference
- 11.30–12.45 ~~Finish the sales report~~
- 12.00–1.15 Check the US contract
- 1.00–2.00 ~~Have lunch with Mr Honda~~
- 1.30–2.30 Have lunch with Mr Honda
- 2.15–3.45 ~~Prepare for the sales conference~~
- 2.45–3.45 Visit the factory with Mr Honda

6 Work with a partner. Ask and answer questions.

1 where / Dieter / work in Britain (Oxford)
Where is Dieter working in Britain?
He's working in Oxford.
2 how many desks / Mr Vennberg / order (660)
3 which department / Mr Honda / visit at the moment (R&D)
4 who / Brian / phone (the agent in Germany)
5 which factory / Mr Tate / visit today (the factory in Manchester)
6 why / Petra / do / Mrs Lawrence's job (because she is on maternity leave)
7 what / Jane and Petra / do / at the moment (some shopping)

7 Complete Petra's letter to an American friend. Put the verbs in the *simple present* or *present continuous*.

I …¹ (be) a trainee with a company called System 7 in Munich. We …² (make) office furniture and …³ (sell) it all over Europe.
At the moment, I …⁴ (work) in the UK office for six months, and I …⁵ (have) a great time here in Oxford. I was in marketing for three months but now I …⁶ (work) in export sales.
It …⁷ (be) hard work, but I …⁸ (learn) a lot here. I …⁹ (know) my English …¹⁰ (get) better here, too!

8 Complete the sentences.

Expressions with 'do' and 'make'

do a job   do (my/your) homework
do a test   do (the/some) shopping

make a plan   make (the) dinner
make (some) coffee   make an appointment
make a mistake

1 Petra *is doing* a different *job* now.
2 Could I … an … to see Mr Tate, please?
3 Jane Stevens often … some … when Lucy Reece has a visitor.
4 Every company has to think about the future and … a business … .
5 Jean Glass sometimes goes out after lunch and … some … in town.
6 In the evening her children … their … and she … the … .
7 I have to … a typing … as part of my interview for this job.
8 I hope I didn't … too many … when I typed the report.

English at work

9 Petra wants to know about System 7 (UK)'s sales this year. Look at the figures and make sentences. Use the table to help you.

Sales of …	are	rising	rapidly	this year.
		falling	slowly	at the moment.
		remaining constant		just now.

Sales of black, three-drawer desks are falling rapidly just now.

	APR–JUN	JUL–SEP	OCT–DEC	JAN–MAR
1 Desk, 3-drawer, black	298	253	174	–
2 Desk, 3-drawer, grey	356	367	353	–
3 Desk, 6-drawer, black	534	542	539	–
4 Desk, 6-drawer, grey	657	671	684	–
5 Chair, medium-back, black	843	976	1075	–
6 Chair, medium-back, grey	954	943	930	–
7 Chair, high-back, red	365	295	234	–

Saying telephone numbers

19334	one-nine-three-three-four
OR:	one-nine-double three-four
5666	five-six-six-six
OR:	five-treble six
70820	seven-oh-eight-two-oh (UK)
OR:	seven-zero-eight-two-zero (USA)

10 Work with a partner. Practise saying these numbers to each other.

| 5437 | 444 55894 | 8629 | 7338883 |
| 788 322 | 509 66 9994 | 544991 | 62066001 |

Now give your partner your home and work telephone numbers.

11 Work with a partner. Practise this conversation.

A System 7 (UK) Ltd, good morning/afternoon.
B Good morning/afternoon. Is that 01865 56767?
A No, sorry, this is 01865 56768.
B Oh, I'm very sorry. Wrong number.

Now partner A look at page 61; partner B look at File 4 on page 159.

Partner B phones you. Pick up the phone and start. Look at the time and say "good morning" or "good afternoon".

	Company name	Time	Right number
1	Smith & Company	15.30	6270
2	Bank of London	09.45	52278
3	C.T.R. Ltd	17.17	511334

Now you phone partner B. Partner B picks up the phone and starts. You want these numbers:

4 4141   5 778760   6 240759

The alphabet and international spelling code

A *ay*	Alpha	J *jay*	Juliette	S *ess*	Sierra
B *bee*	Bravo	K *kay*	Kilo	T *tee*	Tango
C *see*	Charlie	L *ell*	Lima	U *you*	Uniform
D *dee*	Delta	M *emm*	Mike	V *vee*	Victor
E *ee*	Echo	N *enn*	November	W *double-you*	Whisky
F *eff*	Foxtrot	O *oh*	Oscar	X *ex*	X-ray
G *gee*	Golf	P *pee*	Papa	Y *why*	Yankee
H *aytch*	Hotel	Q *queue*	Quebec	Z *zed*	Zulu
I *eye*	India	R *are*	Romeo	(USA *zee*)	

12 Work with a partner. Dictate these abbreviations to each other.

Airlines: BA • JAL • KLM • PIA • SAS • SIA • TWA
Countries/organizations: BRD • CIA • EU • FBI • UN • USA

13 Work with a partner. Look at the international spelling code and then practise these dialogues. Choose names from the list below.

Zukiewicz • Zulikowski • Zulver • Zwanik • Zwosdiak • Zybach • Zydek

A	What name is it, please?		A	Could I make a note of your name, please?
B	It's Mrs Zydek.			
A	Could you spell that, please?		B	My name is Mrs Zydek.
			A	How do you spell that, please?
B	Z…y…d-for-Delta…e…k.		B	Z…y…d-for-Delta…e…k.
A	Sorry, is that k for Kilo?		A	Excuse me, did you say i for India?
B	That's right.		B	No, it's y for Yankee.
A	Thank you, Mrs Zydek.		A	Thank you, Mrs Zydek.

Over to you

14 Work with a partner. Look at the table and learn the phrases.

Telephone phrases (1)

Offering help
Good morning. ABC Ltd. How can I help you?
Good afternoon. ABC Ltd. Can I help you?

Explaining a problem
I'm sorry, but she's out of the office at the moment.
I'm afraid she's on the other line just now.

Offering a return call
Perhaps she can call you back?
Could she call you back?

Offering to take a message
Can I take a message for her?
Would you like to leave a message?

Checking information
Could you spell that, please?
Can I just check that again, please?

Now practise this conversation. Give your own name and number.

OFFICE WORKER AT ABC LTD	CALLER
Good (morning). ABC Ltd. How can I help you?	Hello. Could I speak to (Mrs Hill), please?
Sie erklären das Problem und bieten an, zurückzurufen.	Sie sind einverstanden.
Sie fragen nach dem Namen.	Sie nennen Ihren Namen.
Sie bitten darum, den Namen zu buchstabieren.	Sie buchstabieren Ihren Namen.
Sie überprüfen. Benutzen Sie den Buchstabiercode, falls notwendig.	Sie wiederholen bzw. korrigieren. Benutzen Sie den Buchstabiercode, falls notwendig.
Sie fragen nach der Telefonnummer.	Sie nennen die Telefonnummer.
Sie überprüfen die Nummer.	Sie wiederholen bzw. korrigieren die Nummer.
Sie überprüfen die Informationen nochmals und bedanken sich.	

Focus on grammar

A. Present continuous *(Verlaufsform der Gegenwart)*

Statements	Questions	Negatives
I**'m** working	**am** I working?	I**'m not** working
you**'re** working	**are** you working?	you**'re not** working
he/she/it**'s** working	**is** he/she/it working?	he/she/it **isn't** working
we**'re** working	**are** we working?	we **aren't** working
they**'re** working	**are** they working?	they **aren't** working

SHORT ANSWERS

Yes, I **am**.   No, I**'m not**.
Yes, you/we/they **are**.   No, you/we/they **aren't**.
Yes, he/she/it **is**.   No, he/she/it **isn't**.

'WH' QUESTIONS

Who is she calling?
What is she saying?

❗ begin → begi**nn**ing; get → ge**tt**ing; stop → sto**pp**ing; hav**e** → having; phon**e** → phoning; prepar**e** → preparing; d**ie** → d**y**ing; l**ie** → l**y**ing

> Das **present continuous** zeigt an,
> - dass eine Handlung gerade passiert, *z.B.:* The phone is ringing.
> - oder dass sie vorübergehend und von kurzer Dauer ist, *z.B.:* He's visiting customers in Holland this week.

B. Simple present and present continuous compared

(simple present und present continuous im Vergleich)

SIMPLE PRESENT	PRESENT CONTINUOUS
Petra **works** for System 7 in Munich.	She **is working** for System 7 (UK) this year.
Petra arbeitet (normalerweise) bei System 7 in München.	*Dieses Jahr arbeitet sie (ausnahmsweise) bei System 7 (UK).*
I **watch** TV.	I **am watching** TV.
Ich sehe (manchmal) fern.	*Ich sehe (gerade) fern.*

> Das Verb **to be** und folgende andere Verben werden meistens nicht in der Verlaufsform verwendet:
> *Zustände:* **belong, cost, need, own, seem**;
> *Gefühle:* **hate, like, love, want, wish**;
> *Gedanken:* **believe, feel, know, mean, remember, think, understand**.

8 Delivering goods Warm-up

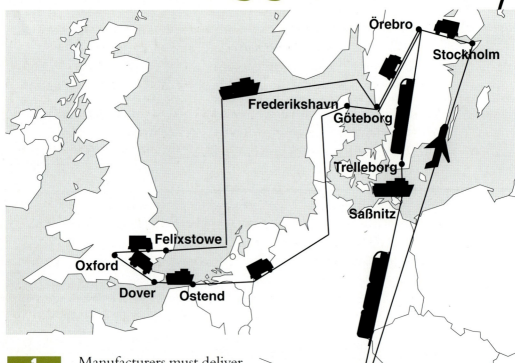

1 Manufacturers must deliver goods cheaply and quickly. This is a complex job, and freight forwarding agencies often do it for manufacturers. You work for a freight forwarding agency. How would you send the following consignments?

1 Transport 100,000 tons of iron ore from Australia to a steelworks in Solingen. *by ship o. by train*
2 Export 10,000 hot-house roses from Israel to Paris in January. *by plane / by truck*
3 Get some secret plans from Düsseldorf to a meeting in Bochum in an hour's time. (There is no fax.) *by courier*
4 Transport 100 new cars from the factory in Munich to Hamburg. *by train or tru*
5 Deliver pizzas from an Italian restaurant to customers at home. *by courier /*

Forms of transport

auf dem Luftweg by air   by plane *mit Flugzeug*
auf dem Schienenweg by rail   by train *mit Zug*   *by Lorry LKW*
auf dem Landweg by road   by courier *Eildienst* by truck *truck* by van *Transporter*
auf dem Seeweg by sea   by ferry *Fähre*   by ship *Schiff*

UNIT 8   64

People at work

🔊 A new delivery schedule

Paul Duval was away, so Dieter handled the Larsen order. The quotation included delivery to Örebro, so Dieter phoned ImpEx, a freight forwarding agency, and spoke to Jason Wright. Jason was in charge of European shipments.

DIETER   Jason, do you remember? You quoted Paul for a large shipment to Larsen Distribution in Sweden last October.

JASON   Yes, we wanted to send the order <u>by sea</u> from Felixstowe to Göteborg.

DIETER   I suppose that's the cheapest method. But when is the next shipment? You see, Larsen now want the order as soon as possible.

JASON   Well, today is Friday, the 22nd. The next sailing is on … er … the 27th. That means arrival in Göteborg on the 29th and delivery to Örebro <u>by rail</u>, probably on the 1st.

DIETER   No, delivery needs to be sooner than that. Larsen need delivery by the 27th. Can we send it <u>by air</u>?

JASON   A big, heavy consignment like that? No, that's the most expensive way! Too expensive. The only way is <u>by road</u>. It's more expensive than <u>by sea</u>, but it's not nearly as expensive as <u>by air</u>.

DIETER   Well, I think the customer will pay.

JASON   All right. I'll handle it. Can the shipment be ready by midday, Monday, the 25th?

DIETER   No problem. What route will it go?

JASON   Across from Dover to Ostend <u>by ferry</u> on Monday night. Then it'll go up the coast to Denmark <u>by road</u>. And then it'll go across from Frederikshavn to Göteborg <u>by ferry</u> on the night of the 26th-27th. Then on <u>by road</u> again next morning. The goods should be there by lunchtime on the 27th.

DIETER   Well, Larsen will certainly be happy to hear that!

At 2 p.m. on the following Wednesday afternoon Mr Vennberg of Larsen Distribution called Petra. "I want to say a very big thank you, to you and your colleagues," he said. "The shipment arrived exactly on time, and we're all very happy here!"

People at work

2 Answer the questions.

1. What was Jason Wright responsible for?
2. How did he plan to send the Larsen order three months before?
3. Why did Dieter ask for a change of plan?
4. Why couldn't the order go by air?
5. How did Jason decide to send the order?
6. How long did the shipment take to reach Larsen?

3 Complete the sentences with these words.

agency • arrangements • export • goods • route • shipment

1. ImpEx Ltd is a freight forwarding … .
2. It helps companies import to the UK and … from the UK.
3. It makes all the … for transport.
4. The company is going to send the … by truck.
5. What is the best … from Oxford to Paris?
6. What kind of … are the trucks carrying?

4 Complete the comparative sentences.

1. The Puma is *faster than* the Rangerider. (fast)
2. The Puma is *less practical than* the Rangerider. (practical)
3. The Micro is … the Rangerider. (slow)
4. The Rangerider is … the Puma. (comfortable)
5. The Rangerider is … the Micro. (fast)
6. The Rangerider is … the Puma. (expensive)
7. The Micro is … the Rangerider. (cheap)
8. The Rangerider is … the Puma. (practical)

5 Complete the superlative sentences.

1. The Micro is *the slowest* of the three. (slow)
2. The Puma is *the least practical* of them all. (practical)
3. The Rangerider … of the three. (comfortable)
4. The Puma … of them all. (fast)
5. The Micro … of the three. (cheap)
6. The Micro … of them all. (expensive)
7. The Micro … of them all. (slow)

MICRO
£7,500

RANGERIDER
£20,000

PUMA
£40,000

6 Form comparative sentences.

(not) as … as = *(nicht) so … wie*

1. Transport by air isn't *as reliable* as transport by sea, but it's *faster*. (reliable) (fast)
2. Transport by sea isn't … transport by road, but it's … (expensive) (slow)
3. Transport by sea isn't … transport by air, but it's … (fast) (cheap)
4. Transport by road isn't … transport by sea, but it's … (cheap) (fast)
5. Transport by sea isn't … transport by air, but it's … (fast) (reliable)

7 Complete the sentences with *too* and one of the words below.

expensive • ill • loud • old • slow • tired • young

too expensive = *zu teuer*
I can do that, **too**. = *Das kann ich* **auch** *(tun)*.

1. They can't send the shipment by sea. It's *too slow*.
2. I can't go to work today. I'm … .
3. We can't buy that car. It's … .
4. We can't do any more today. We're … .
5. Could you turn down the music. It's … .
6. Alan is 63 now, so we shouldn't give him the job. He's … .
7. The children can't stay out until 10.00. They're … .

8 Complete the paragraph. Form *adverbs* from the adjectives in brackets.

The trucks arrived at *exactly* (exact)[1] 8 a.m. The people at System 7 were ready for them and they …[2] (immediate) started loading. The job didn't take as …[3] (long) as Paul expected and the trucks were ready to leave 30 minutes …[4] (early). The drivers ate lunch in the canteen, and they checked the documents …[5] (careful) with Paul. Then they went. The five trucks travelled …[6] (fast) down the M40 motorway towards London. But there were a lot of roadworks on the M25 around London, and this slowed them down …[7] (bad). As the trucks drove south round London, the traffic …[8] (slow) got …[9] (good) than before and they started to move a little …[10] (fast) than an hour earlier. Then they …[11] (final) reached the M20 to Dover. By that time the traffic was moving much …[12] (quick) than before and the five lorries reached the ferry just in time.

English at work

9 At 4.30 one afternoon last week, Anna Wells phoned Petra from a trade fair in Birmingham. She needed some equipment as soon as possible next morning.

Petra found the equipment – some 2.2 metre sections – and they weighed 50 kilograms. Then she called some express delivery companies for these quotes.

TNT

MAXIMUM SIZE: 2 m x 2 m x 2 m
PRICE: £25.00 minimum charge
           up to 5 kg + £1.00 / kg
EARLIEST DELIVERY TIME: 9.00 a.m.
LATEST COLLECTION TIME: 3.00 p.m.

Red Star (British Rail)

MAXIMUM WEIGHT: 50 kg
PRICE: 40-50 kg – £80.00
LATEST COLLECTION TIME: 5.30 p.m.
EARLIEST DELIVERY TIME: 9.00 a.m.

Federal Express

MAXIMUM WEIGHT: 68 kg
MAXIMUM LENGTH: 274 cm
PRICE: 45-50kg – £58.75
LATEST COLLECTION TIME: 4.00 p.m.
EARLIEST DELIVERY TIME: 9.30 a.m.

1. Which company was the cheapest for a 50-kilogram package?
2. Which company was the most expensive for a 50-kilogram package?
3. Which company could not accept a package as long as 2.2 metres?
4. What was the earliest possible delivery time?
5. Which company offered the latest collection time?
6. Which company did Petra choose? Explain why she did not choose the other companies.

10 Now choose the right company for these express packages.

1. Item A will be ready at 3.45 today and it has to arrive before 10.00 a.m. tomorrow. It weighs 65 kilograms.
2. Item B will be ready at 2.30 this afternoon and it has to arrive by 11.00 a.m. tomorrow. It is 1.9 metres long and it weighs 65 kilograms.
3. Item C will be ready at 3.30 p.m. and it has to arrive by midday tomorrow. It is 2.5 metres long and it weighs 63 kilograms.

11 Work with a partner. Look at the table and learn these phrases.

Telephone phrases (2)

Asking to speak to somebody
Hello. May I speak to (Mrs Hill), please. She's on extension 123.
Good morning. Could you give me (Mrs Hill) on extension 123, please?

Connecting a caller
I'll put you through now.
One moment, please.

Explaining a problem
I'm sorry. There's no reply. Can I take a message?
I'm sorry, but the line is engaged at the moment. Would you like to hold?

Giving a message
Could you tell (her) that (her ticket is ready)?
Please tell (her) that (her ticket is ready).

Asking for the caller's name and number
Could I have your name and number, please?
Could you give me your name and number, please?

Giving your name and number
My name is (John Smith) and I'm on (0171 123456).
It's (John Smith) and the number is (0171 123456).

Now complete the conversation. (Look at page 62 to help you.)

RECEPTIONIST	Good morning. Ace Cars Ltd. …[1]?
CALLER	Hello. May I speak to Miss Frost, please? She's …[2] 213.
RECEPTIONIST	I'll …[3].
CALLER	Thanks.
RECEPTIONIST	I'm sorry. The line …[4]. Would you …[5]?
CALLER	No, …[6]. I'm rather busy.
RECEPTIONIST	Can I …[7]?
CALLER	Please. …[8] the documents are ready for signing?
RECEPTIONIST	Yes, certainly. Could I have …[9], please?
CALLER	It's Ken Youde.
RECEPTIONIST	…[10], please?
CALLER	It's Y-o-u-d-e.
RECEPTIONIST	Thank you, Mr Youde.
CALLER	And …[11] 0171 358729.
RECEPTIONIST	So it's …[12] on …[13]. And the message is: …[14].
CALLER	That's it. …[15].
RECEPTIONIST	…[16].

Over to you

12 Work with a partner.
Partner A look at this page; partner B look at File 5 on page 160.

You are a telephone receptionist. Partner B is a caller.
The people s/he wants to speak to are not available. Take the messages.

	Company	Problem
1	Smith Ltd	out of the office
2	Austin & West	line is engaged
3	Banks Company	no reply

Receptionist / Caller

- **Receptionist:** Sie grüßen und bieten Ihre Hilfe an.
- **Caller:** Sie fragen nach einer bestimmten Person und nennen eine Durchwahlnummer.

- **Receptionist:** Sie sagen, dass Sie den/die Teilnehmer/in verbinden werden.
- **Caller:** Sie bedanken sich.

- **Receptionist:** Sie erklären, dass es ein Problem gibt und bieten an, eine Nachricht aufzunehmen.
- **Caller:** Sie sind einverstanden und geben die Nachricht durch.

- **Receptionist:** Sie fragen nach dem Namen und der Nummer des/der Anrufers/in.
- **Caller:** Sie geben die Informationen.

- **Receptionist:** Sie überprüfen die Informationen.
- **Caller:** Sie korrigieren, falls notwendig und bedanken sich.

- **Receptionist:** Sie verabschieden sich.
- **Caller:** Sie verabschieden sich.

Now you are the caller. Partner B is the telephone receptionist. Ask for these people. Give partner B the messages.

	Person	Extension	Message
4	Mrs West	373	meeting is at 2 o'clock, not 3 o'clock
5	Mr Clarke	912	shipment left at 9 a.m. this morning
6	Mrs Carlton	548	documents are ready for signing

Use your own name and number.

Focus on grammar

A. Adjectives and Adverbs *(Adjektive und Adverbien)*

ADJECTIVE	ADVERB
cheap	cheap**ly**
quick	quick**ly**
beautiful	beautiful**ly**

Adjektive beschreiben Substantive; Adverbien beschreiben Verben.
*Um ein Adverb zu bilden, fügt man normalerweise die Endung **-ly** zum Adjektiv hinzu.*

> *Nach den Verben **look**, **sound**, **seem** und **feel** werden Adjektive (also kein **-ly**) benutzt, z.B.* I feel **ill**. – That sounds **expensive**.

B. Irregular Adverbs *(unregelmäßige Formen)*

ADJECTIVE	ADVERB	
fast	fast	*Diese Adverbien haben die gleiche Form wie Adjektive.*
hard	hard	
deep	deep	
high	high	
early	early	
happy	happily	(**-y** → **-ily**)
true	truly	(**e** *wird weggelassen*)
❗ good	**well**	

C. Comparison of adjectives *(Steigerung der Adjektive)*

ADJECTIVE	COMPARATIVE	SUPERLATIVE	
quick	quick**er**	the quick**est**	*(1-silbige Adjektive)*
early	earl**ier**	the earl**iest**	*(2-silbige Adjektive mit Endung **-y**)*
expensive	**more** expensive	the **most** expensive	*(mehrsilbige Adjektive)*
	less expensive	the **least** expensive	
❗ good	**better**	the **best**	*(unregelmäßige*
❗ bad	**worse**	the **worst**	*Formen)*

9 A surprise — Warm-up

MEMO MEMO MEMO MEMO MEMO MEMO

Dear Mrs Reece   6th March

Re: Return of P Hoffmann and D Salter

Please arrange for trainees Hoffmann and Salter to return the weekend of 25th-26th March, and not the weekend of 1st-2nd April, as we previously agreed. Their new jobs in Munich begin on 27th March.

Best wishes

Peter Schliemann

Top Travel
Booking form

Name/s
Hoffmann, Petra Mrs
Salter, Dieter Mr
Flight No.
BA189
Dep
LHR 14.30
Arr
MUC 17.15
Notes
Tickets to System 7 as soon as possible

APRIL 1 Saturday — D & P return to Munich ~~(crossed out)~~

MARCH 25 Saturday — D & P return to Munich

MARCH 26 Sunday

1 Answer the questions.

1. What was Petra's and Dieter's first date of travel to Munich?
2. What is their new date of travel?
3. Who asked for the change? Why?
4. What time is the flight?
5. When will they arrive in Munich?

People at work

🔊 Saying goodbye

It was Petra's and Dieter's last day at System 7 in Oxford. Lucy Reece called Mike Parker and her secretary Jane Stevens for a short meeting.

LUCY Can we check the arrangements for Petra and Dieter? Jane, have the air tickets arrived yet?

JANE Yes, they're here. Petra and Dieter are due to leave Heathrow at 2.30 tomorrow afternoon.

MIKE And I'll take them to the airport. I have a meeting in London tomorrow, so it's on the way.

LUCY That's nice of you. Has somebody bought the things for our surprise party?

JANE Yes, everything is in the kitchen.

LUCY And what have you bought to give them?

JANE Two pen-and-pencil sets. Here you are.

LUCY Great. Now, Mike, could you call everybody in export sales and distribution to the meeting room upstairs at 4.30?

MIKE Yes, OK. And I'll make sure nobody tells Petra and Dieter anything.

LUCY And Jane, could you make the arrangements for the food and drinks?

JANE Yes, sure.

At 4.30 everybody went to the meeting room and Lucy said a few words.

LUCY Thank you all for coming. Now, I don't want to say much. But I think I'm speaking for everybody when I say this to Petra and Dieter: you've been great and we've all enjoyed your visit here. I hope you've enjoyed your time in Oxford as much as we have. And here's a small present for each of you.

PETRA Oh, thank you!

DIETER Thanks very much!

LUCY So … have a good trip back tomorrow. And don't forget about us here in Oxford.

DIETER We certainly won't! Thank you all very much for everything.

PETRA Thank you, everybody. We've had a really good time here.

People at work

2 Answer the questions.

1. What date was the visitors' last day at System 7? (Look at "Warm-up".)
2. What did Lucy want to check with Mike and Jane?
3. What was the "goodbye surprise"?
4. Who was responsible for the food and drinks?
5. What did Lucy give Petra and Dieter?

3 Complete the sentences with these words.

air tickets • arrangements • due • meeting room • responsible • trip

1. The plane is … to leave at 14.30.
2. Jane made the … for the party.
3. The travel agency sent the … to Jane Stevens.
4. The party was upstairs in the … .
5. Jane was … for getting the air tickets.
6. It's a nice day. Let's go for a boat … on the river.

4 Study the lists of things to do.
Then make sentences about them.

Petra and Dieter have given back their office keys to Mike Parker.

Petra hasn't packed her things yet, but Dieter has.

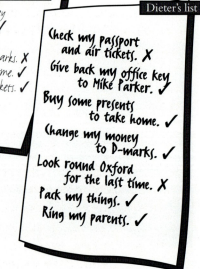

Petra's list
- Give back my office key to Mike Parker. ✓
- Pack my things. ✗
- Change my money to D-marks. ✗
- Buy some presents to take home. ✓
- Check my passport and air tickets. ✓
- Phone my parents. ✗
- Look round Oxford for the last time. ✗

Dieter's list
- Check my passport and air tickets. ✗
- Give back my office key to Mike Parker. ✓
- Buy some presents to take home. ✓
- Change my money to D-marks. ✓
- Look round Oxford for the last time. ✗
- Pack my things. ✓
- Ring my parents. ✓

5 Make questions with *yet*.

1. (Jane / make) the travel arrangements
   Has Jane made the travel arrangements yet?
2. (Petra and Dieter / leave) England
   Have Petra and Dieter left England yet?
3. (the visitors / go) to the airport
4. (Jane / buy) the food and drinks for the party
5. (Jane / find) something to give the visitors
6. (Lucy and Mike / tell) the trainees about the party
7. (Jane / take) the food and drinks upstairs
8. (Petra and Dieter / say) goodbye to their friends

UNIT 9

6 Work with a partner.
Ask the questions in Exercise 5 again. Use these answers and *yes* or *no*.

1 The tickets arrived from the travel agent this morning.
 Yes, she has. The tickets arrived from the travel agent this morning.
2 They're due to leave Heathrow tomorrow.
 No, they haven't. They're due to leave Heathrow tomorrow.
3 Mike will take them to the airport tomorrow morning.
4 They're in the kitchen.
5 She's bought them two pen-and-pencil sets.
6 It's a surprise party.
7 She's still with Lucy and Mike.
8 They said goodbye to them at lunchtime.

7 Form questions from the sentences.

1 Petra has bought some presents. (what?)
 What has Petra bought?
2 Petra and Dieter have stayed in Oxford for six months. (how long?)
3 They have learned a lot of things at System 7 (UK). (what?)
4 They have done different types of work. (how many?)
5 Dieter has visited London a lot. (how often?)
6 Petra has been to other places in England. (where?)
7 She has spent a lot of money on presents. (how much?)

8 Complete the sentences.

anybody • anywhere • everybody (2x) *• everywhere • nobody • nothing • something • somewhere*

1 *Everybody* went to the meeting room.
2 I called three times, but … answered the phone.
3 There's … in the box. What is it?
4 Come here, … . I want to talk to you all.
5 Tony is … in town, but I don't know where.
6 I pressed the switch, but … happened.
7 At first, the visitors didn't know … in Oxford but they soon made friends.
8 I've looked … in the house for my passport, but I can't find it … .

English at work

Telling the time

6.00	six o'clock (in the morning)	six a.m.
6.15	(a) quarter past six	six fifteen a.m.
6.30	half past six	six thirty a.m.
6.45	(a) quarter to seven	six forty-five a.m.
12.00	twelve o'clock	midday/midnight
16.00	four o'clock (in the afternoon)	four p.m.
16.30	half past four	four thirty p.m.

a.m. = von 0.00–12.00
p.m. = von 12.00–0.00

❗ **o'clock** wird nur bei der vollen Stunde verwendet.

Timetables

16.00 = sixteen hundred   16.15 = sixteen fifteen
16.30 = sixteen thirty   16.45 = sixteen forty-five

❗ **o'clock** wird hier nicht verwendet.

9 Work with a partner. Ask for and give these times. Use *a.m./p.m.*

5.00   8.00   9.30   10.15   10.45   11.30   12.00   13.30   14.45   15.15
17.30   18.15   18.45   19.45   20.00   20.15   21.30   23.15   23.45   24.00

Now say them with *in the morning/afternoon/evening/at night*.

10 Work with a partner. Practise this conversation.

A *Excuse me, what time is (the next bus to London), please?*
B *It's at two fifteen (this afternoon).*
A *Could you tell me when (my appointment) is, please?*
B *Yes, it's at eleven thirty-five (tomorrow morning).*

Now partner A look at this page; partner B look at File 6 on page 161.

Partner B asks you questions.   Now ask partner B for these times.
Tell her / him these times.   Write the answers with *a.m.* or *p.m.*

1	10.15	6	my appointment
2	11.30	7	the next bus to London
3	17.45	8	the sales meeting
4	19.50	9	the train to York
5	22.40	10	the concert

UNIT 9

11 Work with a partner. Look at the table and learn the phrases.

> **Telephone phrases (3)**
>
> *Saying what you want*
> I'd like (air tickets for two members of staff), please.
> I need (two single tickets to Munich, on 25th March), please.
>
> *Asking for details*
> Perhaps you could give me the details.
>
> *Offering choices*
> Well, there are (two) choices. You can have … . Or you can take … .
>
> *Making a decision*
> I think (the earlier flight) is better.
>
> *Asking for action*
> Could you (send the tickets to System 7) as soon as possible, please?
>
> *Promising action*
> I'll (book the seats) immediately.
> I'll send them (tomorrow).

Now complete the telephone conversation.
(Also look at pages 62 and 69 to help you.)

ROSIE   Good afternoon. Top Travel. …[1]?
JANE   Hello. It's Jane Stevens here from System 7. I …[2] air tickets for two members of staff, please.
ROSIE   Right. Perhaps you could …[3].
JANE   Yes. I …[4] two single tickets to Munich, on 25th March, please.
ROSIE   Right. Two singles …[5] on the 25th. Fine. What time of day?
JANE   …[6], please.
ROSIE   Afternoon. All right. Could you …[7] for a moment … Well, there are two choices. You …[8] British Airways flight 189 at 14.30 or you …[9] Lufthansa flight 232 at 16.20.
JANE   Mmm. I think the earlier flight is …[10].
ROSIE   Fine, so it's BA flight 189. …[11] the passengers' names, please?
JANE   Yes. They're Miss P Hoffmann and Mr D Salter.
ROSIE   Could you …[12] those names, please?
JANE   Of course. It's Miss P Hoffmann – H…o…double-f…m…a…double-n – and Mr D Salter. S…a…l…t…e…r.
ROSIE   Right. I'll book …[13] immediately.
JANE   And …[14] send the tickets to System 7 …[15]?
ROSIE   I'll …[16] them tomorrow.

Over to you

12 You work for a bus company. It runs bus services between Oxford and Heathrow and Gatwick airports. Look at the timetable and answer the passengers' questions below.

Oxford to Heathrow & Gatwick daily

Oxford Gloucester Green bus station	Heathrow Airport Central bus sta.	Heathrow Airport Terminal † 4	Gatwick Airport South Terminal	Gatwick Airport North Terminal	Oxford Gloucester Green bus station	Heathrow Airport Central bus sta.	Heathrow Airport Terminal † 4	Gatwick Airport South Terminal	Gatwick Airport North Terminal
0200 →	0250 →		0405	0410	1330 →	1440	1500		
0500 →	0610 →		0705	0710	1400 →	1510 →		1605	1610
0630 →	0740	0800			1430 →	1540	1600		
0730 →	0840	0900			1530 →	1640	1700		
0800 →			1005	1010	1630 →	1740	1800		
0830 →	0940	1000			1700 →			1905	1910
0930 →	1040	1100			1800 →	1910	1930		
1030 →	1140	1200			1830 →	1940	SUNDAYS ONLY		
1100 →	1210 →		1305	1310	2000 →	2050 →		2205	2210
1130 →	1240	1300			2030 →	2140	2200		
1230 →	1340	1400							

You should allow sufficient time to check in for your flight. Heathrow airport central bus station is for Terminals 1, 2 & 3. † Use the free shuttle bus to & from Terminal 4.

Christmas & New Year travel:
24 Dec, 31 Dec 2000 to Gatwick & 2030 to Heathrow will not run.
25 Dec No service.
26 Dec, 1 Jan Oxford to Heathrow central bus station 0800, 0930, 1100, 1230, 1400, 1530, 1700, 1830, change at Heathrow for bus to Gatwick

NO NEED TO BOOK AHEAD   PLEASE PAY ON THE BUS

Oxford to	single	3-day return	return
Heathrow	£8	£10	£11
Gatwick	£15	£16	£18

1. What time does the 2.00 p.m. bus reach Gatwick South Terminal?
2. I have to check in at Heathrow Terminal 4 at 11.15. What bus should I catch?
3. I'm going away for three days and I'm flying from Heathrow. How much is the ticket?
4. Do I have to buy a ticket at the bus station?
5. I have to travel on 25 December in the morning. What times are the buses?
6. How long does the bus take from Oxford to Gatwick North Terminal?
7. What time is the last bus to Gatwick in the evening?
8. I have to catch the 11.00 a.m. bus from Oxford, and I have to get to Heathrow Terminal 4. How do I get there?

Focus on grammar

A Present perfect

STATEMENTS	QUESTIONS	NEGATIVES
I've worked	have I worked?	I haven't worked
you've worked	have you worked?	you haven't worked
we've worked	have we worked?	we haven't worked
they've worked	have they worked?	they haven't worked
he's worked	has he worked?	he hasn't worked
she's worked	has she worked?	she hasn't worked
it's worked	has it worked?	it hasn't worked

SHORT ANSWERS
Yes, I/you/we/they **have**.   No, I/you/we/they **haven't**.
Yes, he/she/it **has**.   No, he/she/it **hasn't**.

he's = he is		he has	
she's = she is	ODER	she has	
it's = it is		it has	

'**ve** = have   **haven't** = have not
'**s** = has   **hasn't** = has not

> Merken Sie sich die Wortstellung bei Fragen mit Fragewörtern:
> **Where has** she **been**?   **How long have** you **worked** for System 7?

Man bildet das **present perfect**, indem das Hilfsverb **have** und das Partizip Perfekt benutzt wird. Bei regelmäßigen Verben sind die Formen des Partizip Perfekts und des **simple past** gleich (Grundform + **-ed** oder **-d**).
Unregelmäßige Verben siehe Seite 129

> Das **present perfect** wird häufig mit folgenden Zeitbestimmungen verwendet:
>
> | | |
> |---|---|
> | I've **never/always** flown from Heathrow. | Ich bin niemals/immer von Heathrow geflogen. |
> | Have you **ever** flown from Heathrow? | Sind Sie schon mal von Heathrow geflogen? |
> | He hasn't arrived **yet**. | Er ist noch nicht angekommen. |
> | Has he arrived **yet**? | Ist er schon angekommen? |
> | I've **just** come from Heathrow | Ich bin gerade von Heathrow gekommen. |

B Zusammensetzungen mit some, any, every, no

PEOPLE		THINGS		PLACES	
everybody	jede(r)	everything	alles	everywhere	überall
somebody	jemand	something	etwas	somewhere	irgendwo
nobody	niemand	nothing	nichts	nowhere	nirgendwo
anybody	jemand	anything	etwas	anywhere	irgendwo

10 Going home — Warm-up

- We have to send a fax, but where can we do that? Who do we ask?
- We want to get some duty-free whisky for Dad.
- We haven't got anywhere to stay in London.
- We're flying with British Airways, and we need to tell them we're here.
- We need to buy some Spanish pesetas. Where do we do that?
- We're coming back tomorrow, and we don't want this suitcase until then. What do we do?
- We didn't have time to book a flight before. Where can we do that here?

INFORMATION DESK
BA CHECK-IN DESKS
DUTY-FREE SHOP
EXCHANGE BUREAU
LUGGAGE OFFICE
TICKET SALES OFFICE

1 You hear people say these things at the airport. What should they do? Where should they go?

People at work

On the way home

On the flight home a passenger next to Dieter and Petra started a conversation.

HARRY So, have you guys been on holiday in England?
DIETER No, our company in Munich sent us there last autumn.
PETRA We've been trainees with the UK organization for the last six months.
DIETER Now we're going home. We're starting work at head office on Monday.
HARRY That's nice. What sort of line is your company in?
PETRA We produce office equipment and furniture. We've got operations all over Europe.
HARRY Hey! Are you talking about System 7?
DIETER That's right! How do you know?
HARRY I'm visiting you people on Monday!
PETRA That's amazing!

OFFICE WORLD SUPPLIES

Harry Cross
ASSISTANT DIRECTOR
IMPORT DEPARTMENT

HARRY We're thinking of importing the System 7 range to Canada. Here's my card.
DIETER Hm. Harry Cross. Office World Supplies.
HARRY That's right. We've grown from nothing to sales of eight million dollars in just six years.
PETRA That sounds pretty good.
HARRY I'm meeting your marketing people at 9.00 on Monday. Then I'm meeting the distribution manager, Frau Ziegler, at 11.00. Do you know her?
DIETER She's my new boss!
HARRY No! Well, it's certainly a small world! Tell me, how do I get there from the Hotel Bayern?
PETRA It's about two kilometres by taxi, but you can walk across the park in ten minutes or less. I'll draw a map for you.
HARRY Thanks very much.

At Munich Airport, they all got their luggage and said goodbye.

HARRY Well, it's been nice talking to you. Good luck with your new jobs.
PETRA And good luck with your talks.
HARRY Thanks. Perhaps I'll see you two there at the office.
DIETER I hope so. Goodbye for now.
HARRY Bye.

People at work

2 Answer the questions.

1. When are Petra and Dieter starting work in Munich?
2. How long has Office World Supplies been in business?
3. Who is Harry meeting on Monday?
4. When is his appointment with her?
5. How does Dieter know about her?
6. How far is System 7 from Harry's hotel – a) by taxi, and b) on foot?

3 Complete the sentences.

time • information • work • equipment • furniture • luggage

1. We start ... at 8.30 every morning.
2. We're waiting for ... about Flight 306. Have you heard anything?
3. We needed two trucks to carry all our ... to the new house.
4. Have you got ... to stay for dinner?
5. I want to buy some new computer ... with this money.
6. You can only take twenty kilos of ... on the plane.

4 Match the expressions (1–5) to their meanings (A–E).

1. guys
2. sort of line
3. you people
4. it's been nice talking to you
5. for now

A until the next time
B I've enjoyed our conversation
C people
D your company
E type of work

5 Match the situations (1–6) to the results (A–F).

(1 = E) The parts haven't arrived. That means we can't make the machines.

1. The parts haven't arrived.
2. I've learned a lot of German.
3. Jean has broken her right arm.
4. We've lost our air tickets.
5. You've made a bad mistake here.
6. Mike hasn't finished work.

A That means you must do the work again.
B That means we can't catch our flight.
C That means he can't go home yet.
D That means she can't write.
E That means we can't make the machines.
F That means I may be able to get a job in Germany.

6 Complete the sentences.
Put the verbs into the *simple past* or the *present perfect*.

1 What time *did* the plane *land* last night? (the plane / land)
2 Flight 379 *hasn't arrived* yet. (not arrive)
3 Heathrow Airport first … about 50 years ago. (open)
4 Let's go. They … our flight. (just / call)
5 For her 70th birthday last year, we … Mum a flight on Concorde. (give)
6 … New York? (you / ever visit)
7 We … as fast as possible (drive), but we … there in time for the 8.20 plane. (not get)
8 – … some money into French francs yet? (change)
– Yes, I … to the exchange bureau. (already / be)

7 Explain the arrangements.

Start like this:
On Saturday, Luke is mending his motorbike in the morning. Then in the afternoon, he … And in the evening, …

Luke's sister Jenny and their mother have different plans. They are …

Now explain your own weekend arrangements to a partner.

English at work

8 Work with a partner.
Partner A look at this page; partner B look at File 7 on page 161.

Ask B where these places are: Now tell B where these places are:

1 the information desk   5 Exchange   →
2 the restaurant   6 Hotel reservations ←
3 the taxi rank   7 Post office   ↑
4 the car park   8 Bus station   ↓

A *Excuse me. Which way is / Where's the … , please?*
B *It's straight ahead / to the right / to the left.*

9 Study the chart and complete the statements about the sales of imports.

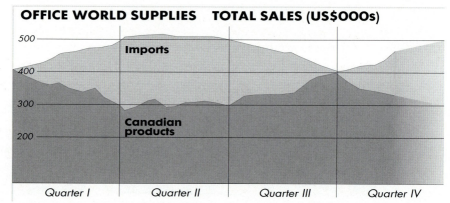

1 In the first quarter sales of imports *grew by one hundred thousand* dollars.
2 In the … quarter sales of imports remained constant.
3 In the … sales … fell by one … dollars.
4 So far this quarter , … have grown … .
5 Since January, … have risen by … .

Now complete the statements about the sales of Canadian products.

6 In the first … sales of … products … by one hundred … .
7 In the … sales of … products … constant.
8 In the … sales … products … by … .
9 So far … quarter, … products … fallen … .
10 Since … , … products … .

What has happened to total sales (Imports + Canadian products) since January?

10 Work with a partner. Look at the table and learn the phrases.

> **Telephone phrases (4)**
>
> Asking for help
> Could you say that again, please?
> Could you speak more slowly, please?
>
> Correcting information
> No. That's not quite right.
> No. That should be … .
>
> Inviting somebody
> Can you join me for lunch tomorrow?
> Would you like to have dinner with me this evening?
>
> Explaining a problem
> That's a nice idea, but I'm not sure right now.
> I'd like to very much, but I must look in my diary first.

Now complete the telephone conversation between Harry Cross and a friend, Bernd Seeberger. (Look at pages 62, 69 and 77 to help you.)

BERND   Seeberger.
HARRY   Hello. Bernd? It's Harry Cross.
BERND   Oh, …¹, Harry! It's good to hear you. Where are you?
HARRY   I'm in Munich on business. Listen. Can …² lunch tomorrow?
BERND   That's a …³, but …⁴ right now. Can I …⁵ back?
HARRY   Fine. I'm staying at the, er, Hotel Bayern.
BERND   Sorry. Could you …⁶, please?
HARRY   The Hotel Bayern.
BERND   Oh, you mean the Hotel Bayern.
HARRY   Sorry. It's in, er, Oettingen Strasse.
BERND   …⁷, please, Harry?
HARRY   Yes, sure. It's O…E…double-T…I…N…G…E…N Strasse.
BERND   Right. And …⁸ number?
HARRY   It's 786 18 25.
BERND   So, …⁹ the Hotel Bayern in Oettingen Strasse.
HARRY   That's right.
BERND   And you're …¹⁰ 786 18 52.
HARRY   No. That …¹¹ 786 18 25.
BERND   Sorry. Right. 786 18 25. I'll call you this evening.
HARRY   Fine. Bye for now.
BERND   Bye.

Over to you

11 Work with a partner.
Draw a line graph (see Exercise 9) to show your company's sales during the last few years. Explain the chart to your partner.

Use these sentences to help you:
Sales have grown from (DM…) to (DM…) in the last five years.
Since 1994, sales have fallen from (DM…) to (DM…).
So far this year, sales have remained constant at (DM…).

Sales grew to (DM…) four years ago.
Sales fell by (DM…) two years ago.
Sales remained constant at about (DM…) last year.

12 Work with a partner and produce this telephone conversation.

YOU (SPEAKING AT THE OFFICE)	A SURPRISE VISITOR
Sie grüßen auf Deutsch.	Sie grüßen auf Englisch.
Sie wiederholen Ihren Gruß, diesmal auf Englisch.	Sie sagen, wo Sie gerade sind, warum Sie sich dort aufhalten und schlagen eine Einladung zum Essen vor.
Sie sind nicht ganz sicher und möchten zurückrufen.	Sie sind einverstanden und nennen den Namen und die Adresse des Hotels.
Sie überprüfen die Informationen.	Sie korrigieren, falls notwendig.
Sie fragen nach der Telefonnummer.	Sie nennen die Telefonnummer.
Sie überprüfen die Information.	Sie korrigieren, falls notwendig.
Sie versprechen, später zurückzurufen, und verabschieden sich.	Sie verabschieden sich.

Focus on grammar

A — Simple past and present perfect compared
(Simple past *und* present perfect *im Vergleich*)

SIMPLE PAST	PRESENT PERFECT
Sales **rose** by 2% **in January**. (*Der Verkauf ist im Januar um 2% gestiegen.*)	Sales **have risen** by 2% **since January**. (*Der Verkauf ist seit Januar um 2% gestiegen.*)
Das **simple past** *wird für ein Ereignis oder eine abgeschlossene Handlung in der Vergangenheit verwendet.*	*Das* **present perfect** *wird für eine Handlung verwendet, die in der Vergangenheit angefangen hat und bis jetzt (***present***) dauert.*

> *Signalwörter (Wann passierte es?):* **yesterday**, **last week**, **two years ago**, **in 1989**, *usw.*
>
> *Signalwörter (Seit wann? Wie lange?):* **since January**, **since 1989**, **so far this year**, *usw.*

Das **present perfect** *wird auch für eine Handlung in der Vergangenheit verwendet, die noch eine Auswirkung auf die Gegenwart (***present***) hat, z.B.*
The parts **haven't arrived yet**.
(*d.h. wir können die Maschinen nicht herstellen*)

B — Future with present continuous
(*Das* present continuous *mit zukünftiger Bedeutung*)

We're starting work **on Monday**.
(*Wir fangen am Montag mit der Arbeit an.*)
I'm meeting Frau Ziegler **at 11 o'clock**.
(*Ich treffe mich mit Frau Ziegler um 11 Uhr.*)

Das **present continuous** *kann auch mit Zeitbestimmungen der Zukunft Pläne und Vereinbarungen ausdrücken.*
Signalwörter: **at 11 o'clock**, **tomorrow**, **next week**, **on Monday** *usw.*

Test 3

1 Explain the sales graph. Use these words.
rise • fall • slowly • rapidly • remain constant

5 months ago | 4 months ago | 3 months ago | the month before last | last month

2 Put the verbs in the *simple present* or the *present progressive*.
Dieter (come) …¹ from the north of Germany, but he (work) …² for System 7 in Munich. System 7 (have) …³ its head office there. Dieter (not work) …⁴ at head office at the moment. He (spend) …⁵ six months with System 7 (UK). "What (you and Petra / do)…⁶ over here in England?" Mark Lester in Production asked him the other day. "We (learn)…⁷ about the business," Dieter replied. "(you / like)…⁸ it here?" Mark asked. "Yes, I (love) …⁹ it here," Dieter said. "And Petra (have)…¹⁰ an interesting time too."

3 Compare the forms of transport.
1. A bus is *slower than* a train. (slow)
2. A train is *more comfortable than* a bus. (comfortable)
3. A plane is … a train. (comfortable)
4. Planes aren't … trains or buses. (convenient = *praktisch*)
5. Airports are a long way from city centres, so the plane isn't … the train or the bus. (convenient)
6. Buses are … trains. (expensive)
7. Trains aren't … planes. (expensive)

4 Make superlative statements about all of the forms of transport.
1. The plane is *the fastest* of them all. (fast)
2. The bus is … of the three. (slow)
3. The bus is also … . (cheap)
4. The train is … . (comfortable)
5. The plane is … . (expensive)
6. The plane is also … . (convenient)

5 Translate these expressions into English.
1. Kann ich ihr etwas ausrichten?
2. Wie ist Ihr Name, bitte?
3. Könnten Sie das bitte buchstabieren?
4. Ich hätte gern Apparat 375, bitte.
5. Einen Augenblick, bitte. Ich stelle Sie jetzt durch.
6. Es tut mir leid, aber die Leitung ist besetzt. Möchten Sie warten?

Test 4

1 Explain the notes in Lucy's diary for today (Tuesday) and tomorrow.
She has an appointment with the managing director at 11.30 this morning. She is going to a sales conference at 10.30 tomorrow morning.

Tues 13th April	Wed 14th April
11.30 a.m. – appointment: managing director	10.30 a.m. – sales conference
2 p.m. – meeting: sales manager	3.30 p.m. – interview new trainees
7 p.m. – dinner appointment: Oxford Training Council	8 p.m. – dinner with reporter from Oxford Times

2 Complete the sentences.
1 *Somebody* wants to talk to Tony, but I can't find him *anywhere* in the office.
2 There isn't ... to do, so can we go home now?
3 I went to the company offices, but ... was there. The place was shut.
4 Steve is ... in France this week, but I don't have a contact number.
5 Check the list again. Are you sure you've done ... ?
6 ... has taken my phone book. Who?!

3 Put the verbs in the correct forms of the *present perfect*.
1 you ... be / to Paris? / ever – *Have your ever been to Paris?*
2 her report. / just / finish / Maria
3 the Italian order / yet? / go out
4 not answer / they / our letter.
5 the power cable? / Tom / where / put

4 Put the verbs in the *simple past* or the *present perfect*.
1 ... the contract late last night. (The directors / sign)
2 I'm sorry to keep you waiting. ... here for long? (you / be)
3 When ... to drive? (Barbara / learn)
4 Lucy is waiting for the letter. ... it yet? (Tony / write)
5 My new room at work is great. ... an office like that for years! (I / want)

5 Translate these expressions into English.
1 Könnten Sie das bitte wiederholen?
2 Könnten Sie etwas langsamer sprechen, bitte?
3 Nein, das ist nicht ganz richtig. Es sollte PBX22 sein, nicht BBX22.
4 Möchten Sie mit mir heute Abend essen gehen?
5 Das würde ich ganz gern tun, aber ich muss zuerst in meinem Terminkalender nachschauen.

11 Back in Munich *Warm-up*

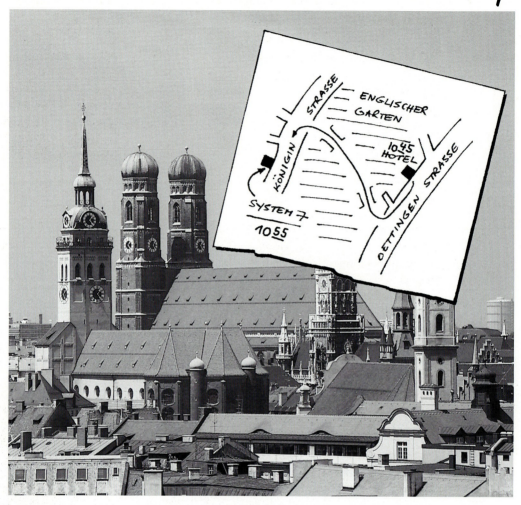

1 Do you remember? Look back at Unit 10. Complete this paragraph.

Harry Cross works for …¹ in …². He wants to import the …³ range of office equipment and …⁴. He has flown to Munich, and he has an …⁵ with Frau …⁶ at …⁷ on …⁸ morning. He is staying at the …⁹ Hotel. …¹⁰ drew the map for him.

2 Look at Petra's map. Describe Harry's walk to System 7.

1 When did he leave the hotel?
2 Where did he go then? (go / walk across / along, turn into / out of)
3 When did he arrive at System 7?

People at work

A new agency

At 8.00 a.m. on Monday morning, Dieter met his new boss, Frau Ziegler, the export distribution manager. They talked about Dieter's new responsibilities for distribution outside Europe. Frau Ziegler then introduced Dieter to the office staff and the warehouse staff. After that Dieter went to his new office. There he started studying the files and the office systems.

Then at the end of the morning his phone rang and Frau Ziegler asked him to come to her office.

ZIEGLER Ah, good, come in. Mr Cross, this is Herr Salter. Herr Salter, Mr Cross.
HARRY   Oh, hi, there, Dieter! Good to see you again. … You see, Mrs Ziegler, Dieter and I have already met.
DIETER We met on the plane on Saturday.
ZIEGLER That's amazing! Well, Herr Salter, Office World Supplies is our new agent in Canada. And Mr Cross, Dieter Salter will be your usual contact. He'll be responsible for dealing with day-to-day matters.
HARRY   Great! I really look forward to working with you, Dieter.
DIETER So do I.
HARRY   You'll have our first order next month.
ZIEGLER So, that's the end of a good morning's work. What about going for lunch now?
HARRY   Good idea!
ZIEGLER You too, Herr Salter.
DIETER Thank you very much.
ZIEGLER Would you like to eat something traditional, Mr Cross?
HARRY   Sure. I like eating local food when I travel.
ZIEGLER Well, Let's go to the Ratskeller. It's a nice day. Would you like to walk, Mr Cross?
HARRY   Fine. I enjoy walking.
ZIEGLER Then, after lunch, you can go sightseeing with Herr Salter if you like. It's worth seeing Munich if you have time. It's an interesting place.
HARRY   Yes, I'd like to do that.

People at work

3 Answer the questions.

1. Who did Dieter meet at 8 a.m.?
2. What did they talk about?
3. After the meeting, what did Dieter do all morning?
4. Why did Frau Ziegler call Dieter to her office?
5. Why will Dieter and Harry often talk in the future?
6. Where did Frau Ziegler and the others go?

4 Complete the sentences.

distribution • export • files • responsibilities • staff • warehouse

1. Germany's … industries sell their products all over the world.
2. Every company needs a … system to get its products to its customers.
3. Before shipments go out, the company keeps them in the … .
4. Dieter is now one of the … at head office in Munich.
5. He is getting a better salary than before, but he also has bigger … .
6. He has to read a lot of … to understand his new job.

5 Work with a partner. Complete the dialogues. Then practise them.

had • has • have (2x) • haven't • 've

AT LUNCH:
ZIEGLER …¹ you ever been to Munich before, Mr Cross?
HARRY Sure, I …² been to Munich quite a few times. I …³ a good friend here, but I …⁴ had time to see him yet.
ZIEGLER Where are you staying?
HARRY Oh, the company …⁵ booked me into the Hotel Bayern. I …⁶ a nice walk across the park to your offices this morning.

could • 'd • should • shouldn't • would (2x)

ZIEGLER …⁷ you like something else, Mr Cross? You …⁸ try the ice-cream here. It's very good.
HARRY Thanks, but I want to lose a few kilos. So I really …⁹ eat any more.
ZIEGLER Well, perhaps you …¹⁰ like some coffee.
HARRY Yes, that …¹¹ nice. …¹² I have an espresso, please?

6 Choose the correct forms to complete the sentences.

1. Would you like *to eat* something traditional? (to eat / eating)
2. I like *eating* local food when I travel. (to eat / eating)
3. We're planning … to the cinema this evening. (to go / going)
4. They managed … the job before the end of the day. (to finish / finishing)
5. Do you mind … on Saturday afternoon next week? (to work / working)
6. Have they finished … the car yet? (to wash / washing)
7. What did they decide … at the end of the meeting? (to do / doing)
8. I'm sorry, but we must go. We can't risk … the plane. (to miss / missing)

7 Complete the sentences with the following expressions with *go*.
Put the verbs in the correct forms.

go: sightseeing • sailing • jogging • swimming • shopping • skiing

1. There was a lot to see in town, so we *went sightseeing* all day.
2. Let's get a boat and … this afternoon.
3. I wanted to run in the London Marathon last year, so I … every day.
4. She always … on Saturday and buys enough to last all week.
5. The water looks great, and we're … ! Do you want to come too?
6. My brother … in Switzerland every January.

8 Put the sentences together. Use *-ing* forms.

1. Don't start any new work today. It's not worth it.
   It's not worth starting any new work today.
2. Visit the museum. It's worth it.
3. Don't try to change the office systems. It's a waste of time.
4. Don't try to change the manager's mind. It's no good.
5. Check the paperwork. You're responsible for it.
6. Don't worry about the exam results. There's no point in it.
7. Don't buy so many clothes. It's a waste of money.

English at work

Asking for directions

Excuse me. | How do I get to the railway station, please?
Could you tell me where the bus station is, please?
Could you tell me the way to the post office, please?

Giving directions

Go out and turn left / right.
Take the first / second turn on the right.

Go along the street until you come to the bridge / traffic lights / …
Go straight ahead as far as the church / river / …

Go past the sports centre / cinema / …
Go over the bridge / under the railway bridge.
Cross the river / railway / road / …

You'll see it opposite the bank.
It's on the left / right.

9 Work with a partner.
Partner A look at this page; partner B look at File 8 on page 161.

You are in the Tourist Information Office.
Ask B for directions to these places:

1. the post office
2. the ABC cinema
3. the River Restaurant
4. the museum
5. the Garden Hotel

Now give B directions.

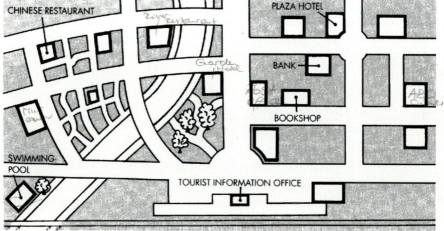

UNIT 11 94

10 Work with a partner.
Use a map of your area, or draw your own map.
Mark on it the following places:

museum • theatre • cinema • church • sports centre • swimming-pool • police station • shopping centre • bank • post office • chemist's • supermarket • your school

Start at your school. Ask for and give directions from place A to place B, place B to place C. Take it in turns to be the visitor.

Excuse me. I'm looking for a chemist's round here. Can you help me?
Yes, there's one in … . (No, I'm sorry. There isn't one.)
Go out and turn … (directions)

11 Practise these job titles.
Frau Ziegler introduced Harry Cross to various members of staff. How did she introduce them in English?

Match their German job titles and the English job titles.

1. Herr Grossmann, Geschäftsführer
2. Frau Haid, Vertriebsleiterin für Europa
3. Frau Pesch, Vertriebsassistentin
4. Herr Zeschky, Leiter der Kundenberatung
5. Frau Brandt, Werbeleiterin
6. Frau Bestermann, Leiterin der Kreditabteilung
7. Frau Müller, Leiterin der Herstellungsabteilung
8. Herr Viebig, Leiter der Versandabteilung

A   production manager
B   dispatch supervisor
C   European sales manager
D   advertising manager
E   managing director
F   assistant sales manager
G   credit control manager
H   customer services manager

Over to you

12 Work with a partner. Look at the table and learn the phrases.

Talking about yourself

I started working here in …
I've worked in this department since …

I'm responsible for distribution to Britain.
I'm responsible for organizing the office.

I enjoy/like telephoning / meeting people / …
I don't like/dislike filing / writing reports / …

One day I'd like to get a job in marketing / work for a big international company.

Asking for more information

Tell me more about …
Sorry, I don't understand.
I'm afraid, I didn't understand.
I didn't follow.

Could you | say more about it?
          | say that again?
          | repeat that?
          | explain that a bit more?

Now ask your partner about herself/himself. Use these questions to help you:

What do you do?
Who do you work for?
Where's that?
How long have you worked there?
What are you responsible for?
What do you like doing best at work?
What do you like doing least?
What sort of job do you want to get one day?

Ask your partner for more information if you don't understand something she/he says.

Now tell your partner about yourself.

Focus on grammar

A -ing form and infinitive (Gerundium und Infinitiv)

Einige Verben stehen mit dem Infinitiv (**to** + Grundform des Verbs), z.B.
Would you **like to eat** something traditional, Mr Cross?
und andere mit dem Gerundium (**ing**-Form), z.B.
I **like eating** local food when I travel.

VERB + TO

agree	zustimmen	**learn**	lernen
arrange	vereinbaren	**manage**	schaffen
attempt	versuchen	**offer**	anbieten
can afford	sich leisten können	**plan**	planen
choose	sich entscheiden	**promise**	versprechen
decide	beschließen	**refuse**	sich weigern
expect	erwarten	**seem**	scheinen
fail	nicht schaffen	**tend**	dazu neigen
hope	hoffen	**want**	wollen

VERB + -ING

avoid	vermeiden	**keep**	weitermachen
delay	aufhalten	**mind ... ?**	ausmachen
dislike	ungern tun	**not mind**	nichts dagegen haben
enjoy	gern tun	**miss**	versäumen
finish	aufhören	**postpone**	verschieben
give up	aufgeben	**practise**	üben
go on	weitermachen	**risk**	riskieren
imagine	sich vorstellen	**suggest**	vorschlagen

Einige Verben können mit dem Infinitiv oder mit der **ing**-Form stehen:

VERB + TO OR -ING

begin	anfangen	**like**	gern haben
continue	fortfahren	**love**	lieben
start	anfangen	**prefer**	vorziehen
hate	hassen		

❗ **would** + **hate** / **like** / **love** / **prefer** + **to**

Die **ing**-Form wird auch mit folgenden Redewendungen verwendet:

It's no use/good ...-ing	Es hat keinen Sinn, ...
It's (not) worth ...-ing	Es lohnt sich nicht, ...
There's no point in ...-ing	Es hat keinen Zweck, ...
It's a waste of time/money ...-ing	Es ist Zeit-/Geldverschwendung, ...

12 A trip abroad — Warm-up

1 London is a good place to buy cheap air tickets. Read the travel company adverts and find the following information.

- the cheapest return flight to New York;
- the cheapest return flight to anywhere in Australia (including Brisbane, Cairns, Melbourne, Perth and Sydney);
- the cheapest round-the-world tour;
- the price of the round-the-world tour with the most stops on the way;
- the cheapest return flight to Los Angeles;
- the cheapest return flight to Hong Kong.

2 Somebody has given you £1,000 for air tickets. Which flight or flights do you want to book? Why?

People at work

The Tokyo trip

Petra's new job was in the marketing department. Her boss, Herr Erhardt, had an immediate job for her – to re-arrange the schedule for his next trip to the Far East. Herr Erhardt needed to stay an extra day in Singapore for a meeting. Petra first called System 7's travel agent. The agent immediately changed the airline reservation and faxed the hotel in Tokyo.

> Ref: Reservation 397/27/5 for Herr K Erhardt of System 7
>
> Herr Erhardt will not arrive on 27th April. He now travels from Singapore on the 28th and his flight arrives at 14.50. He needs a car from the airport and a single room for two nights, 28th-30th April. Please fax your confirmation by return.
>
> Regards

Next, Petra phoned Mr Itoh at Mitsui Corporation in Tokyo.

MITSUI	Moshi-Moshi. Kochira-wa Mitsui Corporation desu.
PETRA	Excuse me. Could you speak English, please?
MITSUI	Yes, who's speaking, please?
PETRA	It's Petra Hoffmann of System 7 in Munich. May I speak to Mr Itoh on extension 315, please.
MITSUI	One moment, please. I'll put you through.
ITOH	Hello. Itoh speaking.
PETRA	Hello, Mr Itoh. It's Petra Hoffmann of System 7 in Munich. I'm calling about your meeting with Mr Erhardt next week. I'm very sorry, but Mr Erhardt can't manage the morning of the 28th. His flight now leaves Singapore on that morning.
ITOH	I see. Well, let me look at my diary … Can he make Thursday morning, the 1st of May?
PETRA	No, I'm afraid he can't make the 1st. He's travelling to Osaka in the evening on the 30th. Could we arrange something else?
ITOH	Well, when would be convenient? If you say a time, I'll try to fit in.
PETRA	Are you free in the afternoon on the 30th?
ITOH	I'm afraid I can't manage the early afternoon, but I can manage a meeting from 3.30 to 5.30.
PETRA	That's fine. Thank you very much, Mr Itoh.
ITOH	No problem.

People at work

3 Answer the questions.

1. What did Petra have to do first in her new job?
2. What date did Herr Erhardt first plan to leave Singapore?
3. Why did Petra have to change his travel dates?
4. When does Herr Erhardt's flight arrive in Tokyo?
5. Who did the travel agent fax in Tokyo, and what did they ask for?
6. When can Mr Itoh meet Herr Erhardt?
7. What is Herr Erhardt doing in the evening on the 30th?

4 Complete the sentences.

appointment • arrange • confirmation • flight • reservation • schedule

1. Could you make a … for a single room for the night of 22nd April?
2. The … from Munich to London only takes an hour and a half.
3. I'd like to make an … to see the manager tomorrow morning, please.
4. We've got a busy … tomorrow. We have to be in Paris at 9 a.m., and we have to be in New York by 5 p.m.
5. Do you still plan to fly on AF 307? We need your … as soon as possible.
6. Could you … a meeting with Mr Newby for Tuesday morning, please?

5 Put the verbs in the correct forms to complete the *if*-sentences.

1. If Herr Erhardt *goes* (go) to Mitsui at 3.30, Mr Itoh *will be* (be) free to see him.
2. Mr Itoh *won't be* (not be) free to see Herr Erhardt if he *arrives* (arrive) earlier than that.
3. If the meeting … (end) at 5.30, Herr Erhardt … (be) able to catch the 7 p.m. train to Osaka.
4. If the meeting … (not finish) on time, he … (miss) that train.
5. But it … (not matter) very much if he … (not catch) that train. He can take a later train.
6. He must travel that evening though. If he … (travel) next morning, he … (lose) part of his working day in Osaka.
7. If he … (not start) work early in Osaka, he … (not complete) all his business by Friday evening.
8. He … (feel) very pleased with himself on his flight home, if he … (manage) to see everybody by Friday evening!

6 Work with a partner. Complete the dialogue. Then practise it.

at • for • from • in • on (2x) • to • until

PETRA IS CALLING MR SUZUKI IN OSAKA:
PETRA   It's about Herr Erhardt's visit, Mr Suzuki.
SUZUKI Oh, yes, let's see. Yes, we're meeting …¹ 10.00 …² 12.00 …³ Wednesday, 30th April.
PETRA   Yes, well, I'm very sorry, but Herr Erhardt now has to stay in Tokyo …⁴ the evening of the 30th. Could he see you …⁵ the 1st?
SUZUKI Well, I've got another meeting …⁶ the morning. But if he comes …⁷ 2 p.m., I'll be free …⁸ two hours then.
PETRA   That'll be fine, Mr Suzuki. Thank you very much.

7 Work with a partner.
Partner A look at this page; partner B look at File 9 on page 162.

Ask B about your travel schedule from London to Stuttgart and back again.

- What date is my flight / return flight to … ?
- What flight number is it?
- What time does it leave / go?
- What time does it arrive / get in?

Write down your travel times.

Now answer B's questions about her/his travel schedule from Düsseldorf to London and back again.

From	Date of Travel	Dep Time	Arr Time	Arrival Airport	Flight No
Düsseldorf	19 Oct	1815	2030	London Heathrow	BA943
London Heathrow	21 Oct	1330	1345	Düsseldorf	BA940

Your flight to … is on … . The flight number is … .
It departs from … at … . It arrives in … at … .

English at work

FROM	BERLIN							FROM	LONDON						
From To	Days 1 2 3 4 5 6 7	Depart	Arrive	Flight number	Aircraft/ Class	Stops		From To	Days 1 2 3 4 5 6 7	Depart	Arrive	Flight number	Aircraft/ Class	Stops
▶	LONDON							▶	NEW YORK (JOHN F. KENNEDY)					
27 Aug-27 Oct	1 2 3 4 5 - -	0640 ①	0830 ① b	BA975	73S/CM	1		Daily		1030 ④	0920	BA 001	Concorde	0
1 Jul - 23 Sep	Daily	0710 ①	0920 ①	BA3115	73S/CM	1		Daily		1100 ④	1335	BA175	747/FJM	0
	Daily	0915	1010 ① b	BA983	73S/CM	0		Daily		1200 ④	1435	BA173	L10/fjm	0
1 Jul - 29 Sep	- - - - - 6 7	1025	1230 ①	BA3011	73S/CM	1		Daily		1415 ④	1650	BA177	747/FJM	0
								Daily		1830 ④	2105	BA179	747/FJM	0

1 Monday 2 Tuesday 3 Wednesday 4 Thursday 5 Friday 6 Saturday 7 Sunday
Concorde - Supersonic Service F First Class J Club World or Business Class
C Club Europe, Super Shuttle or Business Class M Economy Y Economy

Ⓝ Ⓢ Gatwick Terminals
Ⓐ Ⓑ Manchester Terminals
① ② ③ ④ Heathrow Terminals

8 You work at the airline's information desk in Berlin. Answer the passengers' questions.

1 I have to fly to London the day after tomorrow, on Sunday morning. What flights leave for London then and at what times?
2 I want to go to London as early as possible on Thursday, 30th August. What time does the earliest flight leave?
3 And what time does it arrive?
4 I'm flying on Concorde from London next Wednesday. Which terminal does it fly from?
5 I'll be in London next Tuesday, and then I have to go to New York that evening. What time does the evening flight leave for New York?
6 And what time does it get into JFK?

9 You work for an international company in Berlin.
Your American boss gives you this memo.
Use the timetable in Exercise 8 to match the sentence parts.

1 If he catches the 6.40 a.m. plane to Heathrow,
2 If he flies at 9.15 in the morning,
3 If he catches the 10.25 plane,
4 If he flies to New York at 2.15 in the afternoon,

A he'll be late for the meeting at Heathrow.
B he won't have time to get to Manhattan.
C he'll waste time at the airport.
D he'll miss the morning meeting completely.

MEMO MEMO MEMO MEMO MEMO MEMO MEMO

FROM: David Westbrook
SUBJECT: My travel schedule 3rd September

Please find me flights for a trip next Monday, 3rd September to London Heathrow for a short meeting at the airport from 10.00 to 11.00. Then on again to NY in time for a meeting in Manhattan from 17.00 to 18.00. (Please allow 2 hours from arrival at JFK to central New York).
When you find suitable flights, please advise me before you book them.

Now complete the memo. Which flights should you book?

> To: David Westbrook
> Subject: Flights to London & NY, 3rd September
>
> I want to book you on flight …[1] from Berlin to London. This departs at …[2] and arrives at …[3]. I then want to …[4] you on flight …[5] from …[6] to …[7]. This …[8] at …[9] and …[10] at …[11]. If you take these flights, you …[12] be able to go to both …[13].

10 Work with a partner. Practise this conversation.

A Good morning. This is Mrs Wright speaking. Could I make an appointment with Herr Erhardt, please?
B Certainly, Mrs Wright. When?
A On Wednesday afternoon.
B I'm sorry, Herr Erhardt is busy on Wednesday afternoon. Would Thursday at 10 a.m. be all right?

Now partner A look at this page; partner B look at File 10 on page 162.

Call Herr Erhardt's secretary (B) and ask for an appointment. When can Herr Erhardt see you?

	You are	You want to see	When
1	Mr Tornqvist	Herr Erhardt	Tuesday morning
2	Mrs Walters	Herr Erhardt	Wednesday afternoon
3	Mr Bertini	Herr Erhardt	Monday morning

You are now Frau Ziegler's secretary. B calls you and asks for an appointment. Look at the diary and offer the next possible time.

Over to you

Telephone phrases (5)

Asking for an appointment

Could I make an appointment with (…)	this morning/afternoon?
	tomorrow morning/afternoon?
	on Thursday?
	on Friday morning/afternoon?

Explaining a problem

I'm afraid	she's	busy	then.
	he's	not in the office	this morning/afternoon.
		at a conference	tomorrow morning/afternoon.
		in a meeting	on Thursday morning/afternoon.

Making a suggestion

Would	Tuesday morning	at 9.30	be all right?
	this afternoon	at two o'clock	suit you?
	tomorrow afternoon	at half past three	

11 Write your own diary like the one on page 103. Write down some appointments in it. Now work with a partner and arrange a meeting. Use your own names and telephone numbers.

PARTNER A — PARTNER B

- Sie grüßen und bieten Ihre Hilfe an. — Sie grüßen, stellen sich vor und fragen, ob sie einen Termin verabreden können.
- Sie fragen den/die Anrufer/in, wann der Termin sein soll. — Sie sagen, wann Sie den Termin haben möchten.
- Sie erklären, dass es dabei ein Problem gibt und bieten einen anderen Termin an. — Sie sagen, dass dieser Termin bei Ihnen Probleme aufwirft und schlagen einen weiteren vor.
- Sie sind einverstanden und bitten den/die Anrufer/in, seinen/ihren Namen zu buchstabieren. — Sie buchstabieren Ihren Namen.
- Sie fragen nach der Telefonnummer. — Sie nennen Ihre Telefonnummer.
- Sie überprüfen die Informationen. — Sie korrigieren, falls notwendig und verabschieden sich.
- Sie verabschieden sich.

Focus on grammar

A — If sentences type 1 *(if-Sätze Typ 1)*

IF-SATZ	HAUPTSATZ
If you **say** a time,	**I'll try** to fit in.
if + simple present	will + infinitive

If-Sätze (Typ 1) drücken eine Bedingung in der Zukunft aus. Man kann davon ausgehen, dass die Bedingung wahrscheinlich ist. Die Bedingung wird im **if**-Satz ausgedrückt **(simple present)**, die Folge im Hauptsatz **(will-future)**.

❗ *Kein* **will** *im* **if**-*Satz.*

Der **if**-Satz kann entweder vor oder nach dem Hauptsatz stehen. Steht er nach dem Hauptsatz, verwendet man im Englischen kein Komma, z.B. **I'll try** to fit in **if** you **say** a time.

B — Simple present for timetables
(Das simple present *bei Fahrplänen)*

Bei Fahrplänen, Programmen usw. verwenden wir das **simple present**, genau wie im Deutschen.

His flight **leaves** Singapore on the 28th April.
(Seine Maschine startet von Singapur am 28. April.)

Vergleichen Sie aber:
He**'s travelling** to Osaka on the 30th. *(Plan oder Vereinbarung)*
(Am 30. reist er nach Osaka.)

13 A complaint — Warm-up

1 Dieter now has to deal with custumers in markets outside Europe. Copy the table below. Then complete it as well as you can.

Country	Language(s)	Capital City
Japan	Japanese	Tokyo
the USA	...¹	...²
Australia	...³	...⁴
...⁵	Thai	...⁶
...⁷	...⁸	Brazilia
...⁹	...¹⁰	Ottawa

Compare your answers with two or three partners. Talk until you agree. Now try to match the photos to the capital cities.

People at work

A phone call from Canada

The first Office World Supplies order arrived in May and Dieter made the arrangements to supply it by sea a month later. Everything seemed to go well. Then, one day in June, Dieter's phone rang. It was Harry Cross.

DIETER Was the shipment all right, Harry?
HARRY Well, no, I'm afraid not, Dieter. We've got a problem here.
DIETER I'm very sorry to hear it. You'd better give me the details.
HARRY Well, do you remember? We asked for some changes to the light units to meet North American standards.
DIETER Oh, yes, I remember that now.
HARRY Well, there are 250 light units in a separate container that don't have the special parts. They don't meet the standards.
DIETER Oh, no! Look, I'm really sorry about this. I'll talk to Frau Ziegler, and we'll call you back as soon as we can.
HARRY Thanks. Our customer isn't very happy right now, so I hope you can deal with the problem quickly.
DIETER I certainly hope so too.

Dieter tried to talk to Frau Ziegler, but she was away on a business trip, so he called the purchasing department and explained the problem to them. They contacted the supplier – a Japanese company called Mitsumoto – and discussed the matter with them. It was Mitsumoto's mistake, and they were very sorry about it. They wanted to put the matter right as soon as possible. Soon Dieter was able to call Harry back.

DIETER Well, Harry, we've worked out an answer to the problem. The supplier will send a shipment of parts straight to you by air at their expense.
HARRY That sounds good.
DIETER Then, as soon as the shipment reaches you, call me and we'll send an engineer immediately.
HARRY At your expense?
DIETER Yes, of course. And he'll fit the parts for your customer.
HARRY Well, that's excellent. I'm very grateful, so we'll do something to help, too. If you pay the engineer's air fares, we'll pay his local expenses – the hotel, and so on.
DIETER That's really good of you, Harry. We've got a deal!

People at work

2 Answer the questions.

1. When did System 7 send its first shipment to Office World Supplies?
2. What was wrong with some of the lights?
3. Why was it impossible to get Frau Ziegler's help?
4. Who did Dieter explain the problem to?
5. What did Mitsumoto do to solve the problem?
6. What did System 7 do to help?
7. What did Office World Supplies offer to do?

3 Complete the sentences.

attention • containers • deal with • expenses • standards • work out

1. Let's all sit down together and … an answer to the problem.
2. The company pays its sales representatives a good salary, and it also pays all their travel … .
3. All new products have to pass tests to show that they meet the correct … .
4. I don't know what to do about that customer's complaint. Could you … it, please?
5. Send the fax to Mitsumoto for the urgent … of the export manager.
6. The company sends out its export shipments in large … .

4 Complete this letter of complaint.

all of them • a lot of them • half of them • most of them • none of them • some of them

```
We regret to inform you that we were not satisfied
with our order No. OE4978.

Of 300 T-shirts that we ordered, all of them¹ (300)
were unsatisfactory:

…² (280) were the wrong colour;
…³ (210) were the wrong style;
…⁴ (150) were the wrong size;
…⁵ (80) were damaged.

In fact, …⁶ (0) were what we ordered.

We would be grateful if you could send us the
correct items as soon as possible.
```

5 Agree with the speaker. Use the words in brackets and add *so* or *not*.

1 We made some bad mistakes with the last order. (I'm afraid)
   I'm afraid so.
2 I suppose they'll choose another supplier next time. (I hope)
   I hope not.
3 Do you think the order for Spain will be ready by Monday? (I hope)
4 I suppose the production department will have to work through the weekend to get the order ready. (I expect)
5 The new computer system isn't working properly. (I'm afraid)
6 Can the computer company make it work better? (I think)
7 It seems as if sales in America are going to fall. (I'm afraid)
8 And it seems that sales in Europe aren't going to be very good this year. (I believe)

6 Join the sentences with *who*, *which* or *that*.

1 Mitsumoto are the people. They supplied the lights.
   Mitsumoto are the people who (that) supplied the lights.
2 Could I see the lights? Mitsumoto supplied them.
   Could I see the lights which (that) Mitsumoto supplied?
3 Dieter is the person. He will deal with your order.
4 These are the goods. You ordered them.
5 We need a special type of cable. It must meet European standards.
6 Is this the type of cable? You need it.
7 We'd better call the agency. They dealt with the Swedish order last year.
8 Do you remember that Swedish order? We supplied it by road.

7 Work with a partner. Complete the dialogue. Then practise it.

he • him • his • I • it • our • they • we (2x) • you • your

A FEW DAYS LATER HARRY AND DIETER ARE ON THE PHONE:

HARRY   Well, Dieter, the lights are OK now. ...'re[1] all up in ...[2] customer's offices and working.
DIETER ...'s[3] very good to hear that.
HARRY   ...[4] engineer Werner Schwartz has done a really good job.
DIETER Good, but ...'m[5] not surprised. ...[6] chose ...[7] because ...'s[8] very good at ...[9] job.
HARRY   Well, ...'re[10] right, and ...'re[11] taking Werner out for dinner tonight to say thank you.

English at work

8 Work with a partner.

Practise this conversation.

A Have you received an order for 250 office clocks yet, please?
B Yes, but I'm afraid some of them (a lot of them, etc) are broken.
A How many exactly?
B Ten of them.

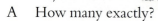

Partner A look at this page; partner B look at File 11 on page 163.

You work in the purchasing department; B works in the stores department.

Ask B about these orders.
What is wrong with them?

```
Order Ref    Description              Qty
OE5047       office clocks            250
OF7589       4-drawer desks           175
OF7601       office chairs (grey)     195
OE4986       desk lamps               360
```

Now you work in the stores department; B works in the purchasing department.

Tell B about the problems with these orders.

```
Order Ref    Description    Qty    Comments
OE4978       tables         10     3 scratched
OF7623       calculators    300    150 missing
OE5101       fax-phones     130    5 cracked
OF7597       shelf units    455    317 the wrong size
```

9 This diagram shows how System 7 deals with orders. Use it to explain what happened after Office World Supplies sent System 7 its first order.

Start like this:

The sales department received an order from Office World Supplies, and the stores department checked the stock. There wasn't enough stock, so the stores department informed the sales department. Then the sales department …

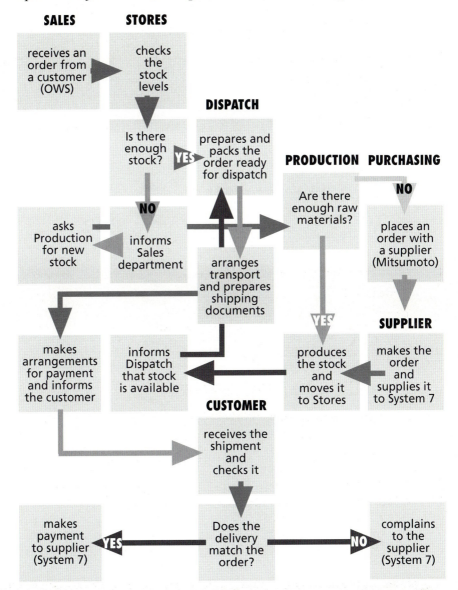

Over to you

10 Work with a partner. Look at the table and learn the phrases.

> **Telephone phrases (6)**
>
> *Making a complaint*
> I'm afraid we've got a complaint (about our order of 13th June).
> I'm afraid there's a problem with our order (number 1234) for …
>
> *Asking for details*
> I'm sorry to hear that. You'd better give me the details.
> I'm very sorry about that. What's the problem exactly?
>
> *Promising action*
> We'll put the matter right / deal with the problem as soon as possible.
> We'll send you (a new consignment) at our expense immediately.

Now produce two conversations. Take turns to be the supplier and the assistant to Harry Cross at OWS.

Supplier	Assistant at OWS
Sie grüßen und bieten Ihre Hilfe an.	Sie grüßen und stellen sich vor.
Sie fragen nach der letzten Lieferung *(everything all right?)*.	Sie antworten, dass es bedauerlicherweise Probleme gegeben hat.
Sie sagen, dass Ihnen das leid tut und fragen nach Details.	Sie bleiben höflich und erläutern die Details.
Sie überprüfen die Details und bestätigen den Fehler.	Sie korrigieren, falls notwendig.
Sie versprechen umgehend eine neue Lieferung.	Sie danken, aber überprüfen nochmal *(at the supplier's expense?)*.
Sie bestätigen.	Sie akzeptieren das, bedanken und verabschieden sich.
Sie entschuldigen sich nochmals und verabschieden sich.	

Ref	Description	Quantity	Complaints
DL42	Desk lamps, black	1,000	about 200 scratched
DL43	Desk lamps, red	1,000	100 missing

Ref	Description	Quantity	Complaints
DC10	Computer disk cases	1,500	about 50 cracked
SC51	Solar cell calculators	500	about 25 broken

Focus on grammar

A — So and not after a verb (So *und* not *im Anschluss an ein Verb*)

SO   I hope you can deal with the problem quickly.
         I certainly hope **so**. *(Ich hoffe es.)*

NOT   Was everything all right with the shipment?
         I'm afraid **not**. *(Leider nicht.)*

So *verwendet man nach folgenden Verben, um einen ganzen Satz zu ersetzen:*

be afraid	*fürchten*
believe	*glauben*
expect	*erwarten*
hope	*hoffen*
think	*denken*
suppose	*annehmen*

(I certainly hope so.
= I certainly hope we can deal with the problem quickly.)

Not *verwendet man bei den oben genannten Verben, wenn sie verneint sind.*
(I'm afraid not.
= I'm afraid everything wasn't all right with the shipment.)

❗ *Merken Sie sich folgende Ausnahmen:* I **don't** expect **so**; I **don't** think **so**.

B — Who, which and that

SUBJEKT   Mitsumoto are the people **who (that)** supplied the lights.

OBJEKT   Could I see the lights **which (that)** Mitsumoto supplied?

Who *wird bei Personen und* **which** *bei Sachen gebraucht.*
That *kann für* **who** *und* **which** *eingesetzt werden.*
Für Personen ist **who** *üblicher.*

C — One of, some of, most of, etc

all of them	*alle*	**a few of them**	*wenige*
a lot of them	*viele*	**one of them**	*eine/r/s*
some of them	*einige*	**none of them**	*keine/r/s*

> *Merken Sie sich folgende Problemfälle:*
> **both of them**   *die beiden*
> **half of them**   *die Hälfte*
> **most of them**   *die meisten*

14 The conference _Warm-up_

There is a plan to build a new motorway through a local beauty spot. You are organizing a public meeting to stop it. Prepare for the meeting with two or three partners.

1 Put these ideas in a better order to produce an agenda for the meeting.

- Discussion point: what can the local community do to fight the plan?
- Welcome people to the meeting.
- Explain what the government is planning to build, and where.
- Agree on a clear plan of action.
- Explain what we, the people of this area, will lose if the government plan goes ahead.

2 Choose a local meeting place. Produce a poster to advertise the meeting. Give the reason for the meeting, the place, the date and the time.

3 What equipment will you need at the meeting? Choose from the following. What will you use this equipment for?

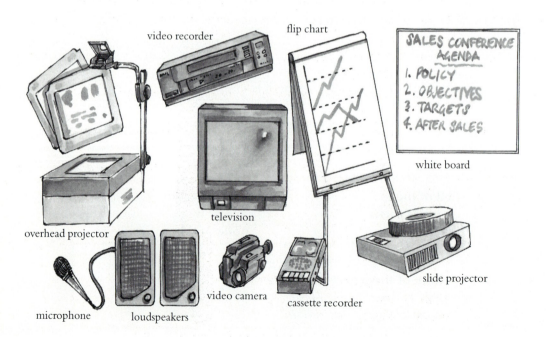

People at work

🎧 Arrangements

Petra had to organize the autumn sales conference. This meant a lot of phone calls and faxes to and from the company's other operations all over Europe – including System 7 (UK). Brian Tate, Petra's old boss, gave his assistant, Lizzie Lawrence, these notes for a phone call to Petra.

> **Conference arrangements**
> Ask for: 4 x 1-hour presentations at different times; a conference room for up to 40 people at each presentation; an overhead projector and white board or flip chart

LIZZIE   Could I speak to Petra Hoffmann, please?
PETRA   Speaking.
LIZZIE   Oh, hello, Petra. It's Lizzie Lawrence here. How are you?
PETRA   Hi! I'm fine. How are you?
LIZZIE   Fine, thanks. Listen. I'm calling about our conference arrangements.
PETRA   Right. Go ahead.
LIZZIE   Well, we want to present the Home Office range to everybody.
PETRA   So what facilities do you need – translators or interpreters?
LIZZIE   No. We're going to do our presentations in each language – German, French, Italian and Spanish.
PETRA   Oh, good! I'm sure everybody's going to be pleased about that.
LIZZIE   So could you give us four one-hour slots in your agenda?
PETRA   Fine.
LIZZIE   And could we have a conference room which is large enough for about 40 people?
PETRA   Well, there's a room that's 10 metres by 8, but I think that's probably too small.
LIZZIE   I agree. It's not big enough, especially as we want to show the product range in the room.
PETRA   We've got another room. It's 20 metres by 10. What about that? It's the size of a large classroom.
LIZZIE   Yes, that sounds just right.
PETRA   Good. Now, what about equipment?
LIZZIE   Right. Could we have an overhead projector and a white board or flip chart?
PETRA   Sorry. Did you say white board and flip chart?
LIZZIE   No. White board or flip chart, please.
PETRA   Fine.
LIZZIE   And now, turning to hotel and eating arrangements …

People at work

4 Answer the questions.

1. Why did Petra have to communicate a lot with System 7's operations in other parts of Europe?
2. What did Lizzie Lawrence call Petra about?
3. How did she know what facilities System 7 (UK) wanted?
4. Why did the UK team plan to present the same products four different times?
5. What size room did Lizzie ask for?
6. What equipment did she ask for?

5 Complete the sentences.

agenda • conference • facilities • interpreter • overhead projector • presentation

1. This … will be very large, so we'll need all the rooms in the hotel.
2. The Royal Hotel's … include several large meeting rooms as well as a business centre.
3. There will be a lot of meetings all day, so the … will be a very full one.
4. Our visitor from Korea doesn't speak any European languages, so we'll need an … .
5. The … will last for 45 minutes and then there will be time for questions.
6. The speaker wants to show some charts, so he needs an … .

6 Work with a partner.
Complete the dialogue with these words. Then practise it.

and • because • but • if • or • so

PETRA IS TALKING TO SILVIE FROM THE FRENCH OFFICE:

SILVIE   We'd like to do a one-hour presentation …¹ three two-hour presentations.

PETRA   Fine. Do you want the main hall …² a smaller room for the one-hour presentation?

SILVIE   My boss wants to talk to everybody, …³ we'll need the main hall, please.

PETRA   Right, …⁴ I don't think we can give you the main hall for the other presentations too. Will it be OK …⁵ we give you a smaller room for them?

SILVIE   Yes, that'll be fine …⁶ our sales team only want to talk to the production people from Munich and Oxford.

7 Join these sentences with *so*. Use *going to*.

so = *da*   **because** = *weil*

1 computer / very old – I / buy / new one
   This computer is very old, so I'm going to buy a new one.
2 photocopier / broken – the company / ask for / another one
3 my office / too small – I / see / my boss / about it
4 delivery / late – we / complain to / supplier
5 sales meeting / at 4 p.m. – Petra / stay late / at the office

Now rewrite the sentences and join them with *because*.
I'm going to buy a new computer because this one is very old.

8 Write the polite requests.

1 At the cinema: you want two tickets. *Could I have two tickets, please?*
2 On the phone: you want the other person to call you back tomorrow.
   Could you call me back tomorrow, please?
3 On the phone to a restaurant: you want to book a table for four people.
4 In the office: you want your colleague to lend you her stapler.
5 In the stores at work: you want a box of computer disks.
6 On the phone to ABC Ltd.: you want to speak to the sales manager.
7 In the street: you want somebody to tell you the way to King's Road.
8 At the airport: you want to change some money into Spanish pesetas.

9 Write questions and answers with *(not) enough* and *too*.

envelope – large/small
door – wide/narrow
cable – long/short
car – cheap/expensive
plane – high/low

Is the envelope large enough?
No, it isn't nearly large enough. It's much too small.

English at work

10 Work with a partner.
Practise this conversation.

A What about a meeting next Monday?
B Well, I'm going to visit the factory in Barcelona then. What about you?
A I'm going to go to a meeting in Paris that day.
B So we can't meet on Monday. What about a meeting on Tuesday?

Now partner A look at this page; partner B look at File 12 on page 163.

Look at your plans for next week. Talk to B and arrange a meeting.

MON Go to a meeting in Paris.
TUE Show some visitors the factory in Wales.
WED Attend a conference in Milan.
THU Work at the office in London.
FRI Visit some customers in Berlin.

Finish like this:
… I'm going to … that day too. So we can meet on … . Fantastic!

11 This year System 7 is going to hold its sales conference in Tenerife. This is the directors' way of saying thank you to the staff for a good year.

Herr Erhardt has given Petra these notes.

```
      Wir brauchen Folgendes:
   - ein Hotel an der Küste, aber nicht in einem
     Touristengebiet
   - Sportanlagen, Schwimmbad usw.
   - Freizeitangebote wie Bootstouren, Angeln,
     Paragliding
   - Einzel- und/oder Doppelzimmer für 200 Personen
   - einen Konferenzsaal für 200 Personen
   - vier kleinere Konferenzräume für jeweils
     bis zu 50 Personen
   - alle Konferenzräume sollten ausgestattet
     sein mit Videogeräten, Overheadprojektoren
     und Schreibtafeln oder Flip-charts
   - vier komplett eingerichtete Büros
     mit eigenem Telefon- und Faxgerätanschluss
```

Now look at page 119. Petra has also got some information from different hotels in Tenerife. They both seem very good, but neither of them is exactly right.

Hotel Santiago

The Hotel Santiago is the ideal place for your next company conference. We offer a quiet, private beach, wonderful sea views and a fine sports club.

Your staff can also enjoy excellent sea fishing and marine sports.

We have single- or twin-bed accommodation for up to 220 people, as well as double bedrooms and family rooms.

We also have excellent conference facilities, with four meeting rooms large enough for 60 people. We can equip them with any type of presentation facility that you need. For parties and larger meetings, you can book our Marine View Restaurant – (maximum 150 people).

Your organization is also welcome to use a desk in the hotel's own main office, and the hotel's telephone and fax communications.

Hotel Vilaflor

The Hotel Vilaflor can offer single accommodation for 300 people, five conference rooms for up to 50 people each, and a hall for up to 250 people.

We can equip all conference facilities with all forms of presentation aids.

We also offer six well-equipped offices with separate phone and fax lines.

The Hotel Vilaflor is only 20 minutes by road from the airport, but it is high up in the hills, away from the hot, noisy tourist areas. We have two swimming pools and excellent sports facilities. We can also arrange day trips to the coast for fishing and other marine sports.

With wonderful views in every direction, you and your team will find this a great place to produce the new ideas your business needs.

Make a list of points for and against each hotel.

Hotel Santiago		Hotel Vilaflor	
For	Against	For	Against
on the coast			

Say what is wrong with each hotel. Use *too* and *not enough*.
The Hotel Vilaflora is too far away from the coast.
The Hotel Vilaflora is not near enough to the coast.

Which hotel should she choose?
She is probably going to choose the Hotel … because … .
She is probably going to decide against the Hotel … because … .

Over to you

12 Work with a partner. Look at the table and learn the phrases.

Telephone phrases (7)

Asking what somebody needs
Do you need office/translation facilities?
Now, what about a meeting room?
Right. Is there anything else you need?

Making requests
Could you give us a white board or a flip chart?
Could we have a room large enough for 40 people?

Agreeing to requests
Fine. / Yes, that's no problem.

Now complete the conversation between Lizzie and Petra about the arrangements for the conference. (Take turns to be each person.)

Hotel and eating arrangements

*Ask for: single-bed accommodation for 24 staff;
vegetarian food for 2 staff members;
evening reception for all conference
participants on 10th July*

LIZZIE	PETRA
Sie erkundigen sich nach den Gegebenheiten von Hotel und Mahlzeiten.	Sie fragen, was Lizzie benötigt.
Sie erklären höflich Ihre Wünsche.	Sie stimmen zu und fragen nach weiteren Wünschen.
Sie sagen, dass das alles sei.	Sie überprüfen die Vereinbarungen.
Sie korrigieren, falls notwendig.	Sie machen deutlich, dass Sie alles verstanden haben.
Sie bedanken sich.	Sie versprechen, eine schriftliche Bestätigung der Vereinbarungen zu schicken.
Sie bedanken sich nochmals und verabschieden sich.	Sie verabschieden sich.

Focus on grammar

A — The future with be going to
(be going to mit zukünftiger Bedeutung)

We**'re going to present** the Home Office range to everybody.
I'm sure everybody**'s going to be pleased** about that.

Be going to + *Verb drückt eine Absicht aus, etwas, das schon entschieden ist.*
We're going to ... *heißt in etwa „wir werden / wir haben vor ..."*

Be going to + *Verb wird auch verwendet, um eine Vorhersage zu machen, die auf Tatsachen basiert, z.B.*
Everybody **is going to be pleased**. (= because the presentation is going to be in each language.)

B — Polite requests with could *(höfliche Bitten mit could)*

Could *wird verwendet,*

- *um nach etwas höflich zu bitten, z.B.*
  Could we have an overhead projector?
- *um nach etwas/jemandem höflich zu fragen, z.B.*
  Could I speak to Petra Hoffmann, please?
- *um jemanden höflich zu bitten, etwas zu tun, z.B.*
  Could you give us four slots?

C — Too and (not) enough

Too
Room 301 is **too large** for one person.
   (Zimmer 301 ist zu groß für eine Person.)
Room 301 is **too small** for five people.
   (Zimmer 301 ist zu klein für fünf Personen.)

Enough
Room 301 is **large enough** for three people.
   (Zimmer 301 ist groß genug für drei Personen.)
Room 301 is **not large enough** for five people.
   (Zimmer 301 ist nicht groß genug für fünf Personen.)

15 A new job — Warm-up

Some English-speaking students are going to visit your college for a few days. Your class are going to have a party for them. You have to prepare some food, as well as drinks.

1 Work with two or three partners. Prepare your ideas for things to eat that are very German. You want to give your visitors a real "taste" of Germany. Write a list.

These expressions will help you:
Let's make …
What about making …?
Why don't we cook …?
I (don't) think we should give them …

After you agree on your menu, each partner should write a copy.

2 Work with a new partner. Take turns to be a visitor. Study your partner's list of food and ask questions like these:

What's this in English?
What do you make it with?
Is it something German?
Where is it from in Germany?

People at work

Something to celebrate

Petra and Dieter received a memo from the managing director of System 7, Herr Grossmann. It invited them to join a special project team, and asked them to a meeting the next day.

They went, and to their surprise they found a group of German and British staff. Their old friend Mike Parker was there. And at the head of the table was Herr Grossmann and their own bosses, Frau Ziegler and Herr Erhardt. Herr Grossmann opened the meeting.

"Ladies and gentlemen, we've chosen you very carefully for a very important new project. And we've brought you together today to tell you about it.

"In fact, this project will be our most important step since we developed the UK sales office into a large organization several years ago. And as we all know, System 7 (UK) now operates very successfully, with its own design and production facilities.

"For several years, we've thought about starting a new manufacturing and distribution company in the Far East. Now, you may know that Herr Erhardt visited Singapore and Japan again last month. On that trip, he made final arrangements to open in Singapore.

"Ladies and gentlemen, we're now going ahead for sure. We're opening the office in January next year. And we're hoping to open the factory in early April. We're going to make our first big move outside Europe, and I know it'll be a big success.

"Now, I very much hope that you will agree to join the team and do this important job. Of course, we can only ask you, and you're the ones who must decide. It's a long way from home and it's a big step to take. But we think you're the people who will do the best job for System 7. All of you are English-speaking, and that's necessary in Singapore. And all of you have shown a lot of talent in your different jobs.

"Now, before you decide, may I say one more thing? If you decide to go, the pay and conditions will be very good."

Dieter and Petra said yes. Mike did too. That evening they went out to a restaurant to celebrate.

"I'm going to need some help," Mike said. "Which are the main courses?"

"Well," Petra said. "Kalbsgulasch is a kind of meat dish, with veal. It's very tasty."

"Bauernschmaus is a traditional dish with pork and dumplings," Dieter told Mike. "It's very filling."

People at work

"But I recommend the Zanderfilet. That's the best, I think," Petra said. "It's a type of fish dish." "All right. I'll have that," Mike agreed. "And for a starter, I recommend the überbackene Champignons. That's mushrooms baked in the oven. They're fantastic here," Dieter said.
The others agreed, and they ordered. A bottle of wine arrived next, and they raised their glasses. "Here's to next year in Singapore!"

3 Answer the questions.

1. What did Herr Grossmann invite Petra and Dieter to do?
2. What is new for the company about the Singapore project?
3. Why has System 7 chosen the people in the project group?
4. Why did Dieter, Petra and Mike go to the restaurant?
5. Why did they drink to next year in Singapore?

4 Complete the sentences.

celebrate • main course • operate • organization • pay and conditions • project • starter

1. The company has chosen a team of people to work on the new … together.
2. The work seems very interesting, and the … are very good too. I think we should take the job!
3. At the moment, System 7 does not … outside Europe.
4. But now the … is going to start a new operation in the Far East.
5. We're going to … the company's new step forward with a big dinner party.
6. I'd like tomato soup as a … , please.
7. Next, we come to the … . Would you like meat or fish?

5 Work with a partner. Complete the dialogue. Then practise it.

are • 'm • 's • was

DIETER AND PETRA ARE IN SINGAPORE; MIKE HAS JUST ARRIVED:

DIETER   Hello again, Mike! How …¹ you? How …² your flight from London?
MIKE   Very tiring, but I …³ fine. And it …⁴ nice to be here.

did • have • haven't • 're • 've

PETRA ...⁵ you been to the hotel yet?
MIKE No, I ... ⁶. I ...⁷ come straight from the airport.
DIETER We ...⁸ going to go back there for lunch soon. Let's go together.
MIKE Good idea. Tell me, when ...⁹ you two arrive?
PETRA Three days ago.

do • doesn't • don't • isn't • will • won't

MIKE How ...¹⁰ you like Singapore?
PETRA Well, we ...¹¹ know the place yet, but it seems fine so far.
Dieter And it ...¹² very big, so it ...¹³ take long to travel round. I guess it ...¹⁴ take long to get to know the place.
MIKE Perhaps that ...¹⁵ be the main problem. It's such a small place.

6 Match the clauses 1–10 and A–J to form sentences.

1 = F

Herr Grossmann has worked for System 7 since the company began in 1970.

1 Herr Grossmann has worked for System 7
2 Since System 7 began in 1970,
3 Before the team members decide to take the Singapore job,
4 If Petra and Dieter are successful in Singapore,
5 Mike Parker was the one
6 The Far East is a rich market,
7 The company chose the members of the project team
8 The new Singapore factory will open in early April
9 System 7 will have to choose a lot of local staff
10 Singapore is the place

A that System 7 finally chose for its first far East operation.
B they need to think about the pay and conditions carefully.
C so System 7 wants to get into it.
D the company has opened offices all over Europe.
E if the company can keep to schedule.
F since the company began in 1970.
G because they are talented and they are also all English speakers.
H they will soon be managers.
I before the factory opens in April.
J who first helped Petra and Dieter in Oxford.

English at work

7 The first meeting of the project team was on 15th September. A week later, Herr Grossmann and Herr Erhardt were back in Singapore. They wanted to check progress and they also gave a press conference.

Study the notes and answer the reporters' questions.

> <u>Three years ago</u>
> System 7 began to plan a new operation somewhere in South-East Asia.
>
> <u>15th-23rd December last year:</u>
> Grossmann & Erhardt travel to Singapore & Indonesia to study suitable places for the new business. They decided on Singapore - better transport links, better-trained workers, better local infrastructure.
>
> <u>19th-24th February this year</u> Grossmann & Erhardt return to Singapore & begin talks with Man Kwong Development Corporation.
>
> <u>22nd May-3rd June</u>
> Erhardt to Singapore & Japan. Completes talks with Man Kwong.
>
> <u>13th June</u> System 7 & Man Kwong sign contracts.
>
> <u>22nd July</u> Work starts on the new office & factory development.
>
> <u>15th September</u> The project team meets at Head Office for the first time.
>
> <u>Early November</u> Herr Erhardt, Mr M Parker & Frau B Ziegler start to interview in Singapore for local office staff.
>
> <u>Late January</u> The project team move to Singapore to open the office at the end of January.
>
> <u>February</u> Mr M Parker & Mr J Patel interview for local production staff.
>
> <u>1st April</u> THE NEW FACTORY OPENS.

1. Herr Grossmann, how long has System 7 wanted an operation in this part of the world?
2. Which countries did you consider?
3. Why did you decide in favour of Singapore?
4. How long did the talks with Man Kwong last?
5. When did you sign the contract?
6. Has work started on the development yet?
7. When did it start?
8. Are you putting together a project group in Europe?
9. What date are the project group arriving in Singapore?
10. When is the office opening?
11. When are you going to interview local people for office jobs?
12. What date are you opening the factory?

8 Work with a partner. Look at the table.

Talking about a menu

Tell me, what's (German name) like?

| It's a | type of
sort of
kind of | fish dish.
meat dish.
casserole
soup | It's very | good.
tasty.
filling.
popular.
traditional. |

One of you is an English-speaking visitor at a restaurant. Study the menu on the right and ask your partner questions about it.

Now change roles. Partner B is the visitor. Ask questions about the menu below.

Vorspeisen

KRABBENCOCKTAIL

TOMATENSUPPE

MATJESFILET

Hauptgerichte

JÄGERSCHNITZEL
MIT POMMES FRITES

HÄHNCHENBRUST
MIT SALAT

GULASCHSUPPE

𝕳𝖔𝖗𝖘𝖕𝖊𝖎𝖘𝖊𝖓

Leberknödelsuppe

Pilzrahmsuppe

𝕳𝖆𝖚𝖕𝖙𝖌𝖊𝖗𝖎𝖈𝖍𝖙𝖊

Forelle „Müllerin" Art

Schweinshaxe
mit Sauerkraut

Bohneneintopf

Rinderbraten
mit Salatbeilage

Over to you

9 What have you done at work or studied at college in the past three years? Write down the correct items from the table below. (Compare what you said about this in Unit 6.)

What have you done best at? What have you done least well at? Mark yourself on a scale from 1 (best) – 5 (least well).

Subjects

book-keeping	telephone work
computer programming	wordprocessing
languages	working with figures
office administration	working with customers
reception work	(other subjects)

Work with a partner. Explain what you have done, what you liked and disliked. Take turns.

I have done book-keeping and office administration. I enjoyed reception work, but I disliked working with figures.

10 What do you want to be one day in the future? Copy the table and tick (✔) the correct job. What don't you want to be? Mark these with an ✘. (Compare what you said about this in Unit 6.)

Jobs

accountant	salesperson
clerical worker	secretary
computer programmer	telephone salesperson
manager	(other jobs)
receptionist	

Work with your partner again. Explain what you want to be / don't want to be, and why. Say why you think you will be good at the job you have chosen. Take turns.

Focus on grammar

Important irregular verbs *(Wichtige unregelmäßige Verben)*

INFINITIV	VERGANGENHEIT SIMPLE PAST	PARTIZIP PERFEKT	
(to) be	was/were	been	sein
become	became	become	werden
begin	began	begun	beginnen, anfangen
break	broke	broken	brechen, kaputtmachen
bring	brought	brought	bringen
buy	bought	bought	kaufen
choose	chose	chosen	(aus)wählen, aussuchen
come	came	come	kommen
cut	cut	cut	schneiden
do	did	done	tun, machen
drink	drank	drunk	trinken
drive	drove	driven	(Auto) fahren
eat	ate	eaten	essen
fall	fell	fallen	fallen
feel	felt	felt	(sich) fühlen
find	found	found	finden
fly	flew	flown	fliegen
get	got	got	bekommen, gelangen
give	gave	given	geben, schenken
go	went	gone	gehen, fahren
have	had	had	haben
hear	heard	heard	hören
know	knew	known	kennen, wissen
leave	left	left	lassen, verlassen
let	let	let	(zu)lassen
make	made	made	machen
meet	met	met	(sich) treffen, kennen lernen
pay	paid	paid	(be)zahlen
put	put	put	stellen, legen, setzen
read	read	read	lesen
ring	rang	rung	klingeln, anrufen
run	ran	run	rennen, laufen, leiten
say	said	said	sagen
see	saw	seen	sehen
sell	sold	sold	verkaufen
sent	sent	sent	schicken, senden
show	showed	shown	zeigen
sing	sang	sung	singen
sit	sat	sat	sitzen
sleep	slept	slept	schlafen
speak	spoke	spoken	sprechen
spend	spent	spent	ausgeben, verbringen
stand	stood	stood	stehen
swim	swam	swum	schwimmen
take	took	taken	nehmen
tell	told	told	erzählen, sagen
think	thought	thought	meinen, denken
understand	understood	understood	verstehen
write	wrote	written	schreiben

Test 5

1 Complete the sentences.
at (2x) • *for* • *from* • *in* • *on* • *past* (2x) • *to* • *until*
1 I was at work … ten hours yesterday.
2 I can't leave the office yet. I can't go … half … five.
3 We showed the visitors round … three … four o'clock.
4 Mr Hammond will arrive in Berlin … midday … Monday.
5 It's a quarter … eight now. The train will be here … fifteen minutes, … eight o'clock.

2 Put the verbs in the correct forms.
MANAGER Well, Bob, you certainly enjoy (use) *using*[1] the computers here. I'd like you (go) *to go*[2] on a computer training course.
BOB Great. I'd love (do) …[3] that. I want to go on (learn) …[4] as much as I can. But when can I go?
MANAGER Well, I can't afford (let) …[5] you go at the moment. We're too busy. I suggest (send) …[6] you next month.
BOB Mm, well, I don't mind (go) …[7] in the first half of next month, but I'm planning (take) …[8] some time off work after that.
MANAGER Then I think you should arrange (join) …[9] a course at the start of next month.

3 Agree with the speaker. Use the words in brackets and add *so* or *not*.
1 I think we'll get the order. (I hope) – *I hope so.*
2 I'm sure GKL won't pay their bill on time. (I'm afraid)
3 It seems to me that we can finish the job today. (I think)
4 I'm sure Barbara won't sign this terrible contract. (I hope)
5 I've heard that the company is starting a new operation in Mexico. (I believe)

4 Put the verbs in the correct forms.
1 Quick! We*'ll be* late for the train if we *don't leave* now. (be / not leave)
2 If we … the train, there … another one for an hour. (miss / not be)
3 We … late for the meeting if we … the later train. (be / catch)
4 If we … at the meeting late, you can be sure we … the contract. (arrive / not get)
5 And the boss … very happy if we … back without that contract! (not be / go)

5 Translate these expressions into English.
1 Entschuldigen Sie. Wie komme ich bitte zum Postamt?
2 Gehen Sie die Straße bis zur Ampel entlang.
3 Sie werden es auf der linken Seite sehen. Gegenüber der Bank.
4 Ich hätte gern einen Termin mit Frau Carter heute Nachmittag.
5 Passt Ihnen morgen Vormittag um 10.30?
6 Leider gibt es ein Problem mit unserer Bestellung vom 15. August.
7 Das tut mir leid. Sagen Sie mir bitte die Einzelheiten.

Test 6

1 Join the sentence parts with the correct words.
and • because • but • if • so • which • who
1 Please complete the form *and* sign it here.
2 In the hotel brochure it says that there's a sports centre … everybody can use.
3 Certainly. … you would like to use the sports centre, please see Juan.
4 Juan is the person … runs the sports centre.
5 The swimming-pool is shut … we're cleaning it.
6 We can play tennis … we can't go swimming.
7 That's OK. It's very hot at the moment, … let's go swimming.

2 Write statements with *too* and *not enough*.
1 These shoes are size 40 and I'm size 42. (they / big) (my feet / big)
They aren't big enough. My feet are too big.
2 I want a really fast car, but this one only does 120kph. (it / fast) (it / slow)
3 Go and help Mrs Evans. She can't carry that case. (it / heavy) (she / strong)
4 Tony isn't very well and he doesn't want to go to the film tonight. He wants to go to bed early. (he / well) (it / late in the evening)
5 You can't make young Rod responsible for the new project!
(he / experienced) (it / big and important)

3 Explain your plans for tomorrow. Use *going to*.
I'm going to meet Mr Lee Yu at Heathrow Airport in the morning.
1 Then …
2 At lunchtime, …
3 In the afternoon,
4 Then in …

> a.m. Heathrow Airport –
>   meet Mr Lee Yu
> Show Mr LY round company –
>   12.00–12.30
> Lunchtime – Directors & Mr LY –
>   lunch – Bell Hotel
> Afternoon – Mr LY have discussions
>   with sales director
> Evening – Lucy and I take Mr LY out
>   – theatre

4 Write the polite requests.
1 At the theatre: you want three tickets.
2 On the phone to another company: you want to speak to the sales manager.
3 On the phone: you want the other person to call you back this afternoon.
4 On the phone: you want to call the other person back tomorrow morning.
5 At the airport: you want somebody to tell you where the Air Iberia check-in desks are.

5 Translate these expressions into English.
1 Ich rufe wegen der Vorbereitungen für die Konferenz an.
2 Wir haben einen Raum für 100 Leute. Wie wäre es mit dem?
3 Das ist genau die richtige Größe.
4 Brauchen Sie sonst noch etwas?
5 Wir könnten ihnen etwas Deutsches zum Essen anbieten.
6 Aus welcher Gegend in Deutschland kommt es?

A   Types of business letter

Example 1: a general enquiry
In this general enquiry an English clothing company asks for some information about sewing machines.

NFF NEW FOCUS FASHIONS LIMITED
47 Fulham Palace Road
London SW6 7HJ

Tel (0171-345) 9861
Fax (0171-345) 7542
Tlx 37965 FOFASH

Industrienähmaschinen Koch GmbH

Rudolf-Diesel-Straße 22
86154 Augsburg
Germany

10 June 19..
Our ref: MH/lg

FOR THE ATTENTION OF THE SALES MANAGER

Dear Sir or Madam

We have received your name and address from the German Chamber of Commerce in Kensington.

Please send us three copies of your current catalogue and price list for industrial sewing machines.

We look forward to hearing from you as soon as possible.

Yours faithfully
New Focus Fashions Limited

Mark Hunter

Mark Hunter
Production Manager

Correspondence

1 Answer the questions.

1 Who is the letter to, and who is it from? *(It is addressed to ... from ...)*
2 Where are New Focus Fashions' offices? *(They are at ... in ...)*
3 How do you know that the writer would like a quick answer to his letter? *(Because he asks Koch to answer ...)*
4 You want to send New Focus Fashions a fax. What is their number? *(It's ...)*
5 Where did New Focus Fashions get the German company's name and address? *(They got it from ...)*
6 Which part of London is the German Chamber of Commerce in? *(It's ...)*

2 Tell your boss in German who the writer of the letter is and what he wants.

3 Answer the questions.

1 You work in the post room at Industrienähmaschinen Koch GmbH. Would you pass this enquiry to ...
   a the accounts department?
   b the export department?
   c the production department?
2 Your boss asks you to answer this enquiry. Would you ...
   a ask NFF what sewing machine they are interested in?
   b send NFF a comprehensive catalogue of all your products?
   c send NFF three sewing machine catalogues and three price lists?

4 Look at NFF's address. Put these London addresses in the right order:

1 England • London SW15 4KL • 16 West Street • United Sound Studios Ltd
2 EC2 7UJ • 15-17 • London • Miss Wendy Hall • Old Essex Road • Windsor Hotel

5 Look at the letterhead and give the short forms of these words or expressions:

1 fax number   4 south-west
2 reference (number)   5 telephone number
3 New Focus Fashions   6 telex number

133

Correspondence

Example 2: a specific enquiry

New Focus Fashions liked what they saw in Koch's catalogue. Mark Hunter decided to ask Koch for an offer. This is what he wrote.

Dear Mrs Klein

Request for quotation

Thank you for sending the catalogues and price lists we asked for so quickly.

We would now be grateful if you could let us have a firm offer for the following machines:

1. 5 (five) RX12 automatic sewing machines with computerized control systems
2. 2 (two) KL 2A button-hole machines
3. 1 (one) TEXPRO software pack

All handbooks to be in English.

Please quote all prices DDP our factory in Bradford on your usual terms.

We would be grateful for a prompt reply because we want to modernize our factory in Bradford by the end of the year.

Yours sincerely
New Focus Fashions Limited

---

6 Answer the questions.

1. Why does Mark Hunter thank Mrs Klein? *(Because she …)*
2. What does the KL 2A machine make? *(It makes …)*
3. What does Mark Hunter say about the handbooks? *(He says that …)*
4. Why are NFF interested in buying new sewing machines? *(Because they want to … in … by …)*

7 Tell your boss in German what kind of sewing machine NFF are interested in. Give him or her as many details as you can.

8 Look at the letter and find the English for these German words:

1. Sehr geehrte
2. Bitte
3. Preisliste
4. dankbar
5. festes Angebot
6. Steuerungssystem
7. angeben
8. baldige Antwort
9. Mit freundlichen Grüßen

Example 3: an offer

Birgit Klein at Industrienähmaschinen Koch in Augsburg wanted to offer New Focus Fashions Ltd good terms. They were a new customer and they were modernizing their plant. This is what she wrote.

INDUSTRIENÄHMASCHINEN KOCH GmbH
Rudolf-Diesel-Straße 22 • D-86154 Augsburg
Telefon (0821) 348907 • Fax (0821) 348908 • Telex 98452

Mr Mark Hunter
New Focus Fashions Limited
47 Fulham Palace Road
London SW6 7HJ
England

Ihr Zeichen	Unser Zeichen	Datum
MH/lg	NFF/148.BK	04.07.19..

OFFER FOR SEWING MACHINES

Dear Mr Hunter

Thank you very much for your enquiry of 28 June, and we are pleased to offer you the following terms for the items you require:

1	5 (five) RX12 automatic sewing machines incl. computerized control systems	DM ... each
2	2 (two) KL 2A button-hole machines	DM ... each
3	1 (one) TEXPRO software pack	DM ...
	Total price	DM ...

As requested, all prices are DDP your factory in Bradford.

These prices are 15% below our list prices and we are also willing to offer a further cash discount of 2% for payment within 15 days of delivery.

We note that all handbooks should be in English.

With the exception of two of the RX12 automatic sewing machines, the consignment can be dispatched immediately from our Munich works by road on receipt of your order. The two remaining machines would be dispatched by 15 September at the latest.

Thank you once again for your enquiry, and we would be delighted to receive an order from you.

Yours sincerely

Industrienähmaschinen Koch GmbH

Correspondence

9 Five of these sentences are wrong. Find the wrong statements and correct them.

1. The letter is to New Focus Fashions in London.
2. Mark Hunter wrote the letter on 4 July.
3. The enquiry was dated 28 June.
4. The letter just gives a very general idea of possible price and terms.
5. All the prices are DDP.
6. The firm offers a discount of 15% on list.
7. The firm is not willing to offer any further discounts.
8. The firm can deliver the complete order immediately.
9. The machines are made in Augsburg.
10. The firm wants to despatch the order by road.

The second sentence is wrong. Birgit Klein wrote the letter, not Mark Hunter. The fourth sentence is wrong, too. The letter is a …

10 Complete the sentences with words or expressions from the lists.

cost • customer • discount • list price • offers • factory • product • terms

1. Sometimes quotations are also called … .
2. Price is more than just the … of a … .
3. A … is when the seller offers the buyer a price lower than the … .
4. Birgit offers NFF such good … because NFF is a new … that is modernizing its … .

cash discount • delivery • dispatched • items offer • payment • requires • road

5. In her letter, Birgit says that Koch is pleased to … the following terms for the … that NFF … .
6. To get the order, Birgit offers NFF a … of 2% if Koch receives … within 15 days of … .
7. The goods will be … from Koch's Munich works by … .

Example letter 4: an order

Mark Hunter was satisfied with Koch's offer. He knew the firm made high-quality products and he was pleased about the 15% discount. New Focus Fashions decided to place the following order.

NFF NEW FOCUS FASHIONS LIMITED
47 Fulham Palace Road
London SW6 7HJ

Mrs B Klein
Industrienähmaschinen Koch GmbH
Rudolf-Diesel-Straße 22
86154 Augsburg
Germany

Tel (0171-345) 9861
Fax (0171-345) 7542
Tlx 37965 FOFASH

Our ref: MH/Lg
18 July 19..

Dear Mrs Klein

ORDER

Many thanks for your offer of 4 July 19... We are pleased to place the following order on the terms you offer:

1. 5 (five) RX12 automatic sewing machines
   incl. computerized control systems   DM ... each
2. 2 (two) KL 2A button-hole machines   DM ... each
3. 1 (one) TEXPRO software pack   DM ...

   Total price   DM ...

We understand from your quotation that all prices are DDP our factory in Bradford and you will despatch the complete consignment less two of the RX12 sewing machines by road on receipt of this order. The two remaining machines will leave your works by 15 September at the latest.

We note that the prices are 15% below list and that you are willing to offer us a cash discount of 2% for prompt payment.

Thank you for dealing with our enquiry so promptly and we look forward to receiving the machines soon.

Yours sincerely
New Focus Fashions Limited

Mark Hunter

Mark Hunter
Production Manager

Correspondence

11 Work with a partner.
Match the questions (1–10) with the answers (A–J). Ask and answer the questions.

1. Which company wrote the letter?
2. What was the date of the quotation?
3. What kind of business letter is it?
4. Where should the firm send the machines?
5. Who pays the transport costs?
6. When will the firm send off the first part of the consignment?
7. What goods will be sent off later?
8. What discount will the buyer get against list price?
9. What must the buyer do to get a cash discount?
10. Why does Mark thank Birgit at the end of the letter?

6. A As soon as it receives the order.
10. B Because she dealt with the enquiry quickly.
8. C Fifteen per cent.
3. D It's an order.
2. E It was 4 July.
1. F New Focus Fashions Limited.
9. G Pay within 15 days of delivery.
5. H The seller.
4. I To Bradford.
7. J Two RX12 sewing machines.

12 Complete the expressions with the right verb.

deal • dispatch • offer • place • submit

1. to … with an enquiry
2. to … a quotation
3. to … a discount
4. to … an order
5. to … a consignment

B Form and layout

Example 1: the form of business letters

Classic Bikes Limited is a British supplier of classic motorbikes. The firm has received a general enquiry from Zweirad-Zentrum-West GmbH in Münster. This is what Harry Todd, the Sales Manager, wrote in reply.

[inside address (address of firm the letter is to)]

[letterhead (address of firm the letter is from)]

CLASSIC BIKES LIMITED
12 Avonmouth Road • Bristol • BR7 8KL
Tel (01272) 189706 • Fax (01272) 754233 • Tlx 97531 CLABI
Registered in England • VAT No. 79522

Mr K Ahrens
Zweirad-Zentrum-West GmbH
Friesenstraße 48
48147 Münster
Germany

[reference] Your ref: CBL/Anf.
Our ref: HT/ws

4 May 19.. [date]

Dear Mr Ahrens [salutation]

Spare parts supply [subject line]

Thank you for your enquiry of 22 April about spare parts for British classic bikes.

We are pleased to let you know that we have a large stock of spare parts for all British bikes, including rare makes such as Matchless and Ariel. Many parts are original but we also supply parts specially manufactured according to original drawings.

We enclose a copy of our trade catalogue and current price list, and we are sure that you will find this interesting reading.

Thank you again for your enquiry and we would be delighted to receive an order from you.

Yours sincerely [complimentary close]

Harry Todd
H Todd [signature block]
Export Sales Manager

Encs: 1x trade catalogue, 1x price list [enclosures]

Correspondence

1 Answer the questions.

1. What is Harry Todd's job?
2. Why has Classic Bikes Ltd written to Zweirad-Zentrum-West?
3. What are "Matchless" and "Ariel"?
4. What does Classic Bikes do when they run out of original parts?
5. What does Harry put in the envelope with his letter?

Punctuation

The example on page 139 shows a letter that doesn't use punctuation for the date, the address, the salutation and complimentary close; it is also possible, but less usual, to use punctuation for these parts of a letter:

> May 4, 19..
>
> Mr K Ahrens,
> Zweirad-Zentrum-West GmbH,
> Friesenstraße 48,
> 48147 Münster,
> Germany
>
> Dear Mr Ahrens,
>
> Yours sincerely,
>
> Encs.: 1x trade catalogue, 1x price list

Letterhead

A letterhead usually shows the company's name and address, its telephone, fax and telex numbers. Sometimes it also says where the firm is registered and its Value Added Tax number.

Inside address

The inside address shows the name and address of the firm you are writing to. This should be exactly the same as the address you use on the envelope.

Mr Richard Smith
49 Courtenay Place
London W1 2RR

Mrs Olive Wendelbaum
1473 Santa Monica Boulevard
Los Angeles, CA 10067

In British addresses the post code comes after the county (in this case London); in American addresses the ZIP code comes after the city name and is separated from it by a comma.

Reference

When you answer a letter from another firm, give the reference of the original letter under **Your Ref:** and your own reference under **Our Ref:**. The reference always at least gives the initials of the person who wrote the letter in capitals and of the person who typed it in small letters, for example **JA/dc**.

Date

You can write dates the following ways:
GB   **13 June 1997**   **13th June 1997**
USA   **June 13, 1997**   **June 13th, 1997**

Never use just numbers, for example **3.10.98**. In Europe this always means **3 October 1998**, but in America and many Asian countries, including Japan, it can mean **10 March 1998**.

Salutation and complimentary close

You start your letter with a **salutation** and finish it with a **complimentary close**.

	SALUTATION	COMPLIMENTARY CLOSE
TO A FIRM	**Dear Sir or Madam**	**Yours faithfully**
	Gentlemen: (USA)	**Yours truly / Truly yours** (USA)
TO A PERSON	**Dear Mr Smith**	**Yours sincerely**
	Dear Mrs Jones	**Sincerely yours/Yours sincerely** (USA)

If you are not sure whether a woman you are writing to is married or not, you can use the form **Ms** instead of **Miss** or **Mrs**.

Subject line

We often use a **subject line** to say in a few words what the letter is about. Always use a subject line when you are writing to a firm for the first time. It will help the firm to decide who should answer your letter.

Signature block

The firm's name often comes directly above the signature and the sender's name and position directly after it.

Enclosures

If you put something into the envelope with a letter, you should write **Enc:** or **Encs:** at the end. This is because in many firms post is opened in the post room and then passed on to the member of staff who will deal with it.

Special notes

Note the meaning of these additions:

(For the) Attention of Ms Helen Jones	*zu Händen von Frau Helen Jones*
Confidential	*Vertraulich*
Private and Confidential	*Persönlich und Vertraulich*
Registered	*Eingeschrieben*
Urgent	*Dringend*

Correspondence

2 Look at pages 139-141 and find the abbreviations for these words:

1 enclosures
2 fax number
3 limited
4 reference
5 telex number
6 Value Added Tax

3 Correct the mistakes. There is one mistake in each address.

1 Miss Susan Snow, Smith Street 3, Ipswich, IP9 7JH
2 New Focus Fashions, 47 Fulham Palace Road, London SW67HJ
3 Pretty Woman Boutique, 10 Beccles Road, NR34 8GH Bungay
4 Mr Kevin Hill, 8 Turner's Lane, London, N3 6BN

4 Write out these dates in a correct form for a business letter.

1 24.8.52   3 9.11.92   5 1/5/95
2 6/4/89   4 31/1/93   6 15.9.97

5 Harry Todd of Classic Bikes plans to visit Klaus Ahrens of Zweirad-Zentrum-West. Put the parts of the letter (A–O) in the correct order.

A Brenda Goodall
B Mr Todd's travel arrangements
C 2 May 19..
D 48147 Münster
E Mr K Ahrens
F Finally, Mr Todd has asked me to tell you how much he is looking forward to seeing you again.
G Dear Mr Ahrens
H Mr Todd's travel arrangements are as follows: he will arrive in Münster by car late on 10 September and he will be staying at the Tecklenburger Hof.
I Friesenstraße 48
J He will come to your offices at 9 a.m. on 11 September: is this time convenient for you?
K Zweirad-Zentrum-West GmbH
L Yours sincerely
M Classic Bikes Limited
N **B Goodall**
O Germany

Example 2: the form of faxes

Zweirad-Zentrum-West was satisfied with their first order from Classic Bikes Limited, and soon other orders followed. The two firms built up a good relationship and before long Klaus Ahrens and Harry Todd were using first names. This fax shows what Harry wrote to Klaus after he had dispatched a consignment of engines to Münster.

CLASSIC BIKES LIMITED
12 Avonmouth Road • Bristol • BR7 8KL
Tel (01272) 189706 • Fax (01272) 754233 • Tlx 97531 CLABI
Registered in England • VAT No. 79522

FAX FAX FAX FAX FAX FAX FAX FAX FAX FAX FAX FAX

To Zweirad-Zentrum -West GmbH, Münster	For Klaus Ahrens	From Harry Todd
Date 24 Oct 19..	Fax-No. 01049/251/128764	Total pages 1 (one)

Subject
Notification of dispatch

Good morning, Klaus

I'm pleased to say that your Order No. 231 for BSA engines has just left Bristol by road via the Channel tunnel. As always, the haulage contractor is Eurotrans 2000. The driver has to make a number of deliveries in Antwerp, Cologne and a couple of places in the Ruhrgebiet, but if he keeps to his schedule he should arrive in Münster by late afternoon on Thursday, 27 October.

Could you please confirm delivery?

All the best, and I hope everything goes all right.

Yours

Harry

If you have not received the number of sheets given above, please contact us immediately on 01272/189706.
Thank you.

Correspondence

6 Read the introduction and the fax on page 143 and fill in the missing words or expressions.

1. Klaus Ahrens works for *the Zweirad-Zentrum in Münster*
2. Harry Todd sent the fax after he had *dispatched* a consignment of … .
4. The lorry is going to Münster via the … . The … is Eurotrans 2000.
5. The driver has to … in several other places on his way to Münster.
6. If the driver … to his … , he will arrive in Münster late on 27 October.
7. At the end of the fax, Harry asks Klaus to … .

Faxes

"Fax" is short for "facsimile", which means "identical copy". A fax machine is a telephone and a photocopier in one. This is why it can transmit identical copies of letters, drawings and photos.

A lot of firms use a printed form for fax messages. When you complete the details at the top of the sheet, make sure that you say who the fax is for, who it is from, the date and – very important – the total number of pages.

Faxes are less formal than business letters. They are often handwritten and they make use of the same kind of language that you would use on the telephone. For this reason, they often open with a spoken greeting like **Good morning**, **Good afternoon** or even simply **Hello**!

The close is also less formal than in letters. Usually people use a friendly expression like **With best wishes** *(Mit den besten Wünschen)*, **With (warmest) regards** *(Mit herzlichen Grüßen)* or **Yours** *(Ihr/e)*, but you can close with just your name.

---

7 Klaus Ahrens asked his secretary to confirm that the engines had arrived in Münster.

Complete her fax to Harry Todd on page 145. Look at Klaus' notes to help you.

- Bestellung-Nr. 231 bestätigen
- LKW gestern Nachmittag (28. Okt.) planmäßig angekommen
- Motoren unbeschädigt und vollständig
- Danke für rasche Abwicklung der Bestellung
- weitere Bestellungen folgen in den nächsten Wochen
- herzl. Gruß

arrived • *as planned* • *Classic Bikes Limited* • *complete* • *confirm* • *confirmation* • *Mr Harry Todd* • *in the next few weeks* • *order* • *quickly* • *undamaged* • *With best wishes* • *29 October*

FAXSCHREIBEN

ZWEIRAD-ZENTRUM-WEST GMBH
Friesenstraße 48
D - 48147 Münster
Tel: (0251) 23 67 34
Fax: (0251) 12 87 64

An: ...¹, Bristol
Für: ...²
Von: M. Nehm (Herr Ahrens)

Datum: ...³
Fax-Nr: 0044/1272/754233
Seiten: 1

Betr.   ...⁴ of delivery

Dear Mr Todd

Mr Ahrens asked me to ...⁵ delivery of our ...⁶ Nr 231. The lorry ...⁷ yesterday afternoon ...⁸. We are pleased to say that the engines were ...⁹ and ...¹⁰.

Thank you for dealing with the order so ...¹¹ and further orders will follow ...¹².

...¹³

Monika Nehm (for Mr Ahrens)

Sollten Sie die o.g. Seitenzahl nicht erhalten haben, setzen Sie sich bitte mit uns unter (0251) 23 67 34 sofort in Verbindung. Danke.

Correspondence

Writing enquiries

GENERAL ENQUIRIES
(Name) is a leading retailer/manufacturer of (products) in Germany.
We have received your name from (the British Chamber of Commerce in Frankfurt).
Please send us three copies of your current catalogue and pricelist, with an indication of trade discounts.

SPECIFIC ENQUIRIES
We would be grateful if you could send us a quotation for the following items: ...
Please quote all prices DDP our (Munich) factory.

Thank you for your trouble and we look forward to hearing from you soon.

8 Look at the table above. Complete this general enquiry with the following words and expressions:

catalogue and pricelist • *fax machines* • *For the attention of* • *heavy lorries* • *we look forward to hearing from you* • *Portsmouth PO6 7JZ* • *Purchasing Department* • *Sir or Madam* • *trade discounts* • *We have received your name from* • *We would be grateful* • *Yours faithfully* • *22 February 19..*

Eltec Communications PLC
Milton Technology Park
...¹

ENGLAND

...² the Sales Manager   ...³

Dear ...⁴
Fax machines for heavy lorries
...⁵ the British Consulate General in Düsseldorf.
Eurotrans GmbH is a leading international haulage contractor with a large fleet of ...⁶. We plan to equip these lorries with ...⁷ to improve communication with the drivers.
...⁸ if you could send us four copies of your current ...⁹ with an indication of your usual ...¹⁰.
Thank you for your trouble and ...11 soon.

...¹²
Eurotrans GmbH
Sieglinde Körte
Sieglinde Körte
...¹³

9 Now write a specific enquiry about Techno 350 fax machines. Address the letter to Ms Helen Shirley, Sales Manager at Eltec. Sign it with your own name. The date is 10 March.

- Start your letter by thanking Eltec PLC for their answer to your general enquiry of 27 February.
- Ask for a quotation for the supply of 25 Techno 350 fax machines. Say they should be suitable for heavy lorries. All instructions must be in German.
- Ask Eltec to quote prices DDP your Dortmund offices and say that you also expect the usual trade discounts.
- Finish your letter by saying that you would like an early reply as your firm wants to carry out the necessary work as soon as possible.

Writing quotations or offers

Further to your enquiry of (17 October) we have pleasure in submitting an offer on the following terms: …
As discussed on the telephone, we can offer you a trade discount of 15% (on list price).
Our usual Terms and Conditions of Business apply.
All prices are quoted DDP your (Bradford) warehouse.
This offer remains valid for (three) months.
If you require any further information, please do not hesitate to contact us.

10 Helen Shirley, the Sales Manager at Eltec PLC, now writes a quotation to Silke Körte at Eurotrans GmbH (address: Hindenburgdamm, 44217 Dortmund). The date is 25 March.

What does Helen Shirley write? Use these notes to help you.

Further to …¹ we have pleasure …² :
25 (twenty-five) Techno 350 fax machines with suitable for heavy lorries …³ DM730.00 each.
Total price …
…⁴ will be in German.
As mentioned in our quotation, we can …⁵ 15% (on list price).
Our usual …⁶ apply.
All prices are …⁷ offices.
…⁸ for (one) month from today's date.
If you require any further information, …⁹

Correspondence

Writing orders and acknowledgements

Orders
Many thanks for your offer of (20 August).
We would be grateful if you could supply the following items at the price agreed.
As agreed, you are willing to allow us a trade discount of 15% (on list price).
Please let us know when the consignment is ready for delivery/shipment.
Thank you for your trouble and we look forward to receiving the goods shortly.
We look forward to receiving your acknowledgement of this order shortly.

Acknowledgements
We acknowledge receipt of your order (No. 1234) of (26 August).
We acknowledge your order for (engine parts) and confirm that we can deliver by the date requested.
Thank you for your order and we are sure that you will be completely satisfied with the consignment.

---

11 Eurotrans was satisfied with Eltec's quotation and decided to place an order. Except for some obvious changes, orders contain the same information as quotations.

Look at Eltec's quotation on page 147 and write Eurotrans' order. Address the letter to Helen Shirley, Sales Manager at Eltec. The date is 12 April.

12 Eltec acknowledged receipt of Eurotrans GmbH's order.

Put the sentences (A–D) from the acknowledgement in the correct order. Now add the following items and write the complete letter:

date (18 April) • inside address • subject line • salutation • complimentary close • signature block

A We can confirm that the consignment will be despatched within the next few days.
B We acknowledge receipt of your order for removable fax machines for heavy lorries dated 12 April.
C Thank you for your order and we are sure you will be completely satisfied with the machines.
D We will fax you the details on departure.

C Complaints & reminders

Example 1: a complaint about late delivery

If you need to make a complaint about late delivery, don't forget that there are a lot of reasons why things can go wrong: some things just happen. It helps to be polite and helpful rather than aggressive.

Becker & Schürmann GmbH, has ordered a consignment of colour monitors. Unfortunately, the consignment did not arrive on the due date.

Industrieweg 17 • 90439 Nürnberg • Tel (0911) 44 97 17 • Fax (0911) 54 22 03

Mrs Fiona Carter
Essex Digital Limited
32-34 Victoria Road
Romford
Essex RM1 8GT

England

Datum	Ihr Zeichen	Unser Zeichen CK/ht
9 November 19..		

Our Order No. 3497 of 8 October 19..

Dear Mrs Carter

The above order for colour monitors has still not arrived, although delivery was due on 6 November.

Please look into what has happened and let us know when we can expect the consignment.

We would be very grateful if you could do this immediately because we have some urgent orders from our own customers that we would like to fill as soon as possible. Thank you for your trouble and we are sure that we will hear from you very soon.

Yours sincerely
Becker & Schürmann GmbH

Christel Klein
Christel Klein
Buying Department

Correspondence

Example 2: a reply to a complaint about late delivery

When she got Christel Klein's letter, Fiona Carter of Essex Digital Ltd was worried because the monitors had left Romford several days before. She got in touch with the haulage contractor to find out what had happened. She then sent Christel this fax.

Dear Ms Klein

I was worried to hear that your Order No. 3497 has still not arrived, because it left our stores on 3 November. Although this was a little late, the driver assured us that it would definitely arrive in Nuremberg by 6 November at the latest. I was glad to hear this at the time because of bad weather in the North Sea.

I have now spoken to the haulage contractor and they told me their lorry was indeed badly held up first by ferry delays and then by flooding in Holland. On top of that, their driver also had mechanical trouble with his lorry.

However, I am very pleased to tell you that the consignment will definitely be with you any minute now if it has not already arrived.

I am very sorry about this delay, but I'm sure that your customers will understand that these things sometimes happen.

With best regards

---

1 Answer the questions.

1 When were the monitors due for delivery in Nuremberg?
2 Why does Christel Klein ask Essex Digital for an immediate answer?
3 Why was Fiona Carter worried when she got Christel's letter?
4 When did the driver expect to arrive in Nuremberg?
5 What three things held up the lorry between Romford and Nuremberg?
6 When does Fiona expect the consignment to arrive in Nuremberg?

Example 3: a complaint about incomplete delivery

Asahi Clothing Supplies Ltd of Seoul, South Korea makes zip-fasteners and buttons for the clothing industry. New Focus Fashions Ltd of London has ordered some zip-fasteners from Asahi, but when the consignment arrives one item is missing.

When we checked the above consignment of zip-fasteners against your delivery note we found that it was incomplete.

Seven hundred and fifty (750) white plastic zip-fasteners were missing. As the package has not been opened since leaving Seoul, the fasteners were obviously not put into the package in the first place.

Could you please send us the missing fasteners as soon as possible? Perhaps you could send them air freight direct to our Bradford factory as our production department there needs them immediately.

Example 4: a reply to a complaint about incomplete delivery

Asahi Clothing Supplies Ltd looked into the question of the missing zip-fasteners and then sent NFF this fax.

```
Thank you for your letter of 22 July and we are very sorry
that the white plastic zip-fasteners were left out of the
consignment.

This was due to an oversight in our packaging department.
We have now improved our final inspection procedures so
that such mistakes cannot happen again.

We have already dispatched the zip-fasteners by air freight
to Manchester Airport and have arranged for them to be
delivered to Bradford by express courier at our expense.
```

2 Answer the questions.

1. What were the missing zip-fasteners made of?
2. How does NFF know that the mistake happened at Asahi's factory?
3. Why does NFF ask Asahi to send the fasteners direct to Bradford?
4. What has Asahi done to make sure that such mistakes do not happen again?
5. How will the zips be transported from Manchester to Bradford?
6. Who pays the transport costs?

Correspondence

Example 5: a reminder

Some customers do not pay their invoices on time. Often a friendly telephone call is enough, but sometimes it is necessary to send out written reminders.

Lisa Morse at Essex Digital Ltd. sent this reminder to a shop in Norfolk.

ESSEX DIGITAL LIMITED

32-34 Victoria Road Romford, Essex
RM1 8GT

Tel (01708) 763301
Fax (01708) 763302

```
Mr M Richards
Data Computers Ltd
16 North Norfolk Business Park
Cromer, Norfolk
NR12 9VK
```

Your ref:
Our ref: LM/lm
31 May 19..

Dear Mr Richards

Our invoice of 12 March 19..

We are sure that you have forgotten the enclosed invoice for £934.45, or perhaps you have simply mislaid it.

As we say in our Terms and Conditions of Business, all invoices are payable within 28 days of receipt of goods and our prices and discounts are calculated on this basis.

As payment is now more than two weeks overdue, we would be grateful if you could arrange for the outstanding amount to be paid within the next few days.

If you have paid the invoice in the meantime, we would like to thank you and we know that you will ignore this reminder.

Yours sincerely
ESSEX DIGITAL LIMITED

Lisa Morse
Lisa Morse (Miss)
Accounts Department

Enc: invoice (copy)

Example 6: a reply to a reminder

Because of tough competition Data Computers was having problems of payment. Mr Richards wrote back to Lisa Morse and asked her for more time to pay the invoice.

Dear Miss Morse

Your invoice of 12 March and letter of 31 May

We are very sorry that we have not written to you before about the above invoice, but we hoped that we would be able to settle it in the meantime.

The "price war" in the retail computer market has caused prices to fall through the floor. Some big suppliers are now offering complete machines at prices below those that we must charge just for the parts. For this reason, business has been very slow.

We are doing all we can to pay our way in difficult times, but we cannot possibly settle your invoice in full immediately. We hope, therefore, that you will agree to accept payment in three monthly instalments, two of £310.00 each and a final instalment of £314.45.

We would be most grateful if you could agree to this, and enclose the first monthly instalment with this letter.

Yours sincerely

3 Answer the questions.

1. What was the date of Essex Digital's original invoice to Data Computers Ltd?
2. What are Essex Digital's terms of payment?
3. Why does Lisa enclose a copy of the invoice with her first reminder?
4. Why didn't Mr Richards write to Essex Digital earlier?
5. What effect has the price war had on the retail computer market?
6. How does Mr Richards want to pay Essex Digital's invoice?

Correspondence

Writing complaints and replies to complaints (1)

COMPLAINTS ABOUT DELAYS IN DELIVERIES
We are writing about our Order No. (1234) which has still not arrived.
As our own customers are waiting for delivery we are extremely dissatisfied with the situation.
Please let us know at once when we can expect delivery.
We are sure you understand our position and look forward to an improvement in future.

REPLYING TO COMPLAINTS ABOUT DELIVERY
We were sorry to hear that your Order No. (1234) has still not arrived.
The consignment left our (Krefeld) factory on time and the delay has been caused by bad weather / a breakdown / a strike on the cross-channel ferries.
I can now inform you that the consignment will arrive (in London) on 22 March / next week at the latest.
I am sorry about the delay, but I am sure that you / your customers will understand that these things sometimes happen.

A customer has written to Essex Digital Ltd to complain about a delay in delivery. Complete the complaint.

are writing about • from our own customers • for your trouble • has still not arrived • hear from you • let us know • order of 10 February • was due • would be grateful • Yours sincerely • 18 March 19..

…¹

Dear Mrs Carter

Our …² for 200 modems

We …³ our order No. 35286/XD for 200 modems.
The consignment …⁴ although delivery …⁵ on 15 March.

We …⁶ if you could …⁷ as soon as possible when we can expect delivery. We have some large orders …⁸ that we urgently need to fill.

Thank you …⁹ and we are sure that we will …¹⁰ soon.

…¹¹

Frank Higgins

154

5 Now complete Fiona Carter's reply to Mr Higgins at Connors Computers Ltd (address: 54 O'Donnell Street, Dublin, Ireland). Sign the letter with Fiona Carter's name. The date is 21 March.

Use these notes to help you.
- very sorry that we haven't dispatched modems
- delay caused by strike at components factory in Toulouse
- inform them that strike now over; order dispatched yesterday
- apologise for the delay, but these things sometimes happen

Writing complaints and replies to complaints (2)

COMPLAINTS ABOUT INCOMPLETE DELIVERY
On checking the consignment (against your delivery note), we found that it was incomplete. (The white plastic zip fasteners) are missing.
We would be grateful if you could send us the missing items as soon as possible.

REPLYING TO COMPLAINTS ABOUT DELIVERY
We regret that your Order No (1234) was incomplete.
The mistake was caused by an oversight in our packing/despatch department.
We have already arranged for the missing items to be forwarded to you (by air freight) at our expense.

6 When a boutique checked a delivery of fashion belts it found that some items were missing so the manager sent a fax to the supplier.

Translate the German words into English and then use the English words to complete the fax.

We confirm receipt of our ...¹ (Bestellung) for fashion belts, but when we checked the ...² (Sendung) against your ...³ (Lieferschein) we found that 30 coloured ...⁴ (Gürtel) were missing. The package was ...⁵ (unbeschädigt), so a ...⁶ (Fehler) was obviously made at your ...⁷ (Fabrik).

We would be ...⁸ (dankbar) if you could send the missing belts ...⁹ (so bald wie möglich). This is rather ...¹⁰ (dringend) as they are needed for our own ...¹¹ (Kunden).

Thank you for your ...¹² (Mühe), and we look forward to receiving the belts soon.

Correspondence

7 You work for the supplier of fashion belts. Reply to the manager of the boutique by fax. Use these notes to help you:

- Danke für Ihr Fax vom 18. November.
- Es tut uns leid, dass unsere Sendung von Gürteln nicht vollständig war. Dies ist aufgrund eines Versehens in unserer Versandabteilung passiert. Sie können sicher sein, dass solche Fehler nicht wieder vorkommen werden.
- Wir haben schon veranlasst, dass die fehlenden 30 Gürtel auf unsere Kosten per Kurierdienst versandt werden. Sie werden morgen bei Ihnen eintreffen.

Writing reminders and replies to reminders

REMINDERS
We are writing about our invoice of (20 December), which we are sure you have overlooked.
As we say in our Terms and Conditions of Business, all invoices are payable within 28 days of receipt.
We would be grateful if you could arrange payment of the outstanding invoice within the next few days.
If you have settled the invoice in the meantime, we thank you for your payment and are sure that you will ignore this reminder.

REPLYING TO REMINDERS
We are sorry that we were not able to settle the above invoice when it was due.
The recession has caused serious financial problems (in the computer industry).
We are certain that we will be able to pay the outstanding invoice by (30 June) at the latest.
We would like to suggest that we pay the invoice in (four) monthly instalments of (£250) each.
Thank you for your help, and we will do our best to pay the invoice by the agreed date.

8 Complete this reminder to Mrs Jane Carr of Hampstead Boutique (address: 37A Highgate Road, London NW16 9ST. Use these notes from your boss, Frau Kempitz. Look at the table above and the model letter on page 152 to help you.

Invoice No. 19374/HB
- invoice for £297.50 (10 August): overlooked or mislaid?
- terms: 28 days; prices calculated on this basis; therefore request cheque within next few days
- if invoice paid, ignore reminder

Yours, etc

9 Translate the German words and expressions into English and then use them to complete this reply to a reminder.

begleichen • Bestellungen • Betrag • bis spätestens • Einzelhändler • fällig • möchten vorschlagen • Monatsraten • Rate • Rechnung • Rezession • Scheck • sicher • Umsatz • zustimmen

---

Dear Mr Hartmann

I am writing to you about your …¹ for DM12,854 of 19 November. We are sorry that we were not able to …² the amount by the date …³.

As a …⁴ of luxury goods, we are suffering particularly badly because of the …⁵. All our customers are placing smaller …⁶ than usual, and this has led to a big drop in …⁷.

We …⁸ that we pay the outstanding invoice in three …⁹. We enclose a …¹⁰ for the first …¹¹ of DM4,300 and hope that you …¹² to this suggestion.

We thank you for your help, and we are …¹³ that we will be able to pay the outstanding …¹⁴ by 31 March …¹⁵.

Yours sincerely

Pairwork files

FILE 1 UNIT 2, EXERCISE 12

Partner A asks you about two things on the equipment list. Look at this memo and tell partner A what you need.

> Things I need
> biros   staples   paper clips   notepads

Now ask partner A about two things on the equipment list. What things does partner A need?

```
Equipment list

1 biros         pencils
2 staples       paper clips
3 notepads      files
```

FILE 2 UNIT 2, EXERCISE 15

Here are nine people and their jobs. Listen to partner A's sentences.

Now read these sentences to partner A.

1. The receptionist is between the filing clerk and the mailroom supervisor.
2. The secretary is on the left of the assistant personnel manager.
3. The production manager is between the marketing manager and the mailroom supervisor.
4. The assistant personnel manager is between the secretary and number four.

Who is on the left of the marketing manager?

158

FILE 3 — UNIT 5, EXERCISE 11

Act these conversations. Make notes to help you first, if necessary.

1 Partner A is a receptionist; partner B is a visitor. Partner A begins:

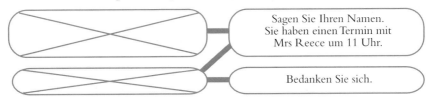

Sagen Sie Ihren Namen.
Sie haben einen Termin mit Mrs Reece um 11 Uhr.

Bedanken Sie sich.

2 Partner A is a visitor; partner B is Petra Hoffmann. Partner B begins:

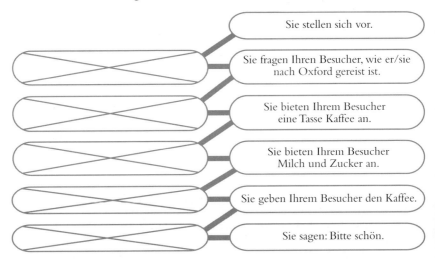

Sie stellen sich vor.

Sie fragen Ihren Besucher, wie er/sie nach Oxford gereist ist.

Sie bieten Ihrem Besucher eine Tasse Kaffee an.

Sie bieten Ihrem Besucher Milch und Zucker an.

Sie geben Ihrem Besucher den Kaffee.

Sie sagen: Bitte schön.

FILE 4 — UNIT 7, EXERCISE 11

You phone partner A. Partner A picks up the phone and starts. You want these numbers:

1. 6207
2. 62278
3. 512334

Now partner A phones you. Pick up the phone and start. Look at the time of day and say "good morning" or "good afternoon".

	COMPANY NAME	TIME	RIGHT NUMBER
4	Hardy & Jones	15.05	1441
5	Grand Hotel	11.50	887760
6	P.R.D. Ltd	17.20	240795

Pairwork files

FILE 5

UNIT 8, EXERCISE 12

Partner A is a telephone receptionist. You are a caller. Ask for these people. Give partner A the messages. Use your name and number.

	PERSON	EXTENSION	MESSAGE
1	Mr Martin	281	his plane leaves at 7 a.m. tomorrow
2	Mrs Green	585	Dr Steiner wants a meeting as soon as possible
3	Mrs Young	379	Mr Wilson wants the sales figures

RECEPTIONIST — **CALLER**

- Sie grüßen und bieten Ihre Hilfe an. — Sie fragen nach einer bestimmten Person und nennen eine Durchwahlnummer.
- Sie sagen, dass Sie den/die Teilnehmer/in verbinden werden. — Sie bedanken sich.
- Sie erklären, dass es ein Problem gibt und bieten an, eine Nachricht aufzunehmen. — Sie sind einverstanden und geben die Nachricht durch.
- Sie fragen nach dem Namen und der Nummer des/der Anrufers/in. — Sie geben die Informationen.
- Sie überprüfen die Informationen. — Sie korrigieren, falls notwendig, und bedanken sich.
- Sie verabschieden sich. — Sie verabschieden sich.

Now you are the telephone receptionist. Partner A is the caller.
The people s/he wants to speak to are not available. Take the messages.

	COMPANY	PROBLEM
1	Blacksons & Co	on a business trip
2	Whytes Ltd	no reply
3	James & James	line is engaged

FILE 6 UNIT 9, EXERCISE 10

Ask partner A for these times. Write answers with *a.m.* or *p.m.*

Now partner A asks you some questions. Tell her/him these times.

1 next train to Oxford
2 marketing meeting
3 the last interview
4 plane to Munich
5 TV programme

6 9.15
7 11.20
8 14.00
9 15.35
10 20.15

FILE 7 UNIT 10, EXERCISE 8

Tell A where these places are:

Now ask A where these places are:

1 Information desk →
2 Restaurant ←
3 Taxi rank →
4 Car park ↑

5 the exchange bureau
6 the hotel reservations desk
7 the post office
8 the bus station

A *Excuse me. Which way is / Where's the ... , please?*
B *It's straight ahead / to the right / to the left.*

FILE 8 UNIT 11, EXERCISE 9

You are in the Tourist Information Office. Give A directions.

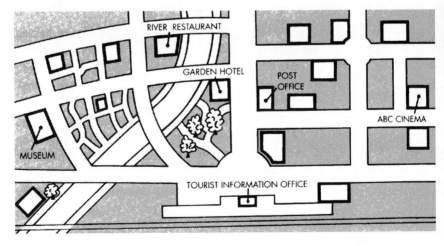

Now ask A for directions to these places:

6 the Chinese restaurant
7 the best bookshop
8 the swimming-pool
9 the bank
10 the Plaza hotel

161

Pairwork files

FILE 9 UNIT 12, EXERCISE 7

Answer A's questions about her/his travel schedule from London to Stuttgart and back again.

From:	Date of Travel	Dep Time	Arr Time	Arrival Airport	Flight No
London Heathrow	24 Oct	2230	2145	Stuttgart	LH 4127
Stuttgart	27 Oct	1900	2020	London Heathrow	LH 4128

Your flight to … is on … . The flight number is … .
Your flight departs from … at … . It arrives in … at … .

Now ask A about your travel schedule from Dusseldorf to London and back again.
- What date is my flight / return flight to … ?
- What flight number is it?
- What time does it leave / go?
- What time does it arrive / get in?

Write down your travel times.

FILE 10 UNIT 12, EXERCISE 10

You are Herr Erhardt's secretary. A calls you and asks for an appointment. Look at the diary and offer the next possible time.

Now call Frau Ziegler's secretary (A) and ask for an appointment. When can Frau Ziegler see you?

	YOU ARE	YOU WANT TO SEE	WHEN
1	Mrs Ward	Frau Ziegler	Monday morning
2	Mrs Honda	Frau Ziegler	Tuesday morning
3	Mr Rossi	Frau Ziegler	Wednesday afternoon

FILE 11 UNIT 13, EXERCISE 8

You work in the stores department; A works in the purchasing department. Tell A about the problems with these orders.

```
Order Ref      Description        Qty     Comments
OE5047         office clocks      250     10 broken
OF7589         4-drawer desks     175     39 dented
OF7601         office chairs      195     195 the
               (grey)                     wrong colour
OE4986         desk lamps         360     27 bent
```

Now you work in the purchasing department; A works in the stores department. Ask A about these orders. Write down the problems.

```
Order Ref      Description        Qty
OE4978         tables             10
OF7623         calculators        300
OF5101         fax-phones         130
OE7597         shelf units        455
```

FILE 12 UNIT 14, EXERCISE 10

Look at your plans for next week. Talk to A and arrange a meeting.

MON Visit the factory in Barcelona.
TUE Work at the office in London.
WED Spend the day at the Frankfurt Trade fair.
THU Have talks in New York.
FRI Attend a conference in Berlin.

Finish like this:
  … I'm going to … that day too. So we can meet on … . Fantastic!

Chronologisches Wörterverzeichnis

Dieses Wörterverzeichnis zeigt alle Wörter in der Reihenfolge ihres ersten Auftretens. Neue Vokabeln aus Correspondence A werden ab Unit 6 vorausgesetzt bzw. aus Correspondence B ab Unit 11.
AE = amerikanisches Englisch; *BE* = britisches Englisch

UNIT 1

6 trainee [treɪ'niː] — Auszubildende(r)
head office [ˌhed 'ɒfɪs] — Zentrale
confirm [kən'fɜːm] — bestätigen
flight [flaɪt] — Flug
(With) best wishes [wɪð best 'wɪʃɪz] — Alles Gute
personnel manager [ˌpɜːsə'nel 'mænɪdʒə] — Personalleiter(in)
complete [kəm'pliːt] — vervollständigen
company ['kʌmpənɪ] — Gesellschaft, Firma
7 producer [prə'djuːsə] — Produzent, Hersteller
office furniture [ˈɒfɪs 'fɜːnɪtʃə] — Büromöbel
sales office ['seɪlz ˌɒfɪs] — Verkaufsbüro
factory ['fæktərɪ] — Fabrik, Werk
organization [ˌɔːgənaɪ'zeɪʃn] — Unternehmen
Ltd. (Limited) ['lɪmɪtɪd] — GmbH
assistant [ə'sɪstənt] — Assistent(in)
Excuse me. [ɪk'skjuːz mɪ] — Entschuldigung.
That's right. [ðæts 'raɪt] — Das stimmt.
Pleased to meet you. [ˌpliːzd tə 'miːt ju] — Es freut mich, Sie kennen zu lernen.
tell [tel] — sagen
food [fuːd] — Essen
in charge [ˌɪn 'tʃɑːdʒ] — verantwortlich sein
personnel [pɜːsə'nel] — Personal
How do you do? [haʊ dʊ jʊ 'duː] — Guten Tag/Abend., Angenehm.
just [dʒʌst] — einfach
informal [ɪn'fɔːml] — ungezwungen, nicht förmlich
let's (let us) [lets] — lassen Sie uns
look around [ˌlʊk ə'raʊnd] — ansehen, umsehen
quite [kwaɪt] — ziemlich, ganz
over there [ˌəʊvə 'ðeə] — da drüben
run [rʌn] — leiten, führen
production manager [prə'dʌkʃn ˌmænɪdʒə] — Produktionsleiter(in)
8 match [mætʃ] — zuordnen
desk [desk] — Schreibtisch
sell [sel] — verkaufen
product ['prɒdʌkt] — Produkt, Erzeugnis
practise ['præktɪs] — üben
trade fair ['treɪd ˌfeə] — Handelsmesse
expensive [ɪk'spensɪv] — teuer
perhaps [pə'hæps] — vielleicht
business ['bɪznɪs] — Geschäft, Firma
do business — ins Geschäft kommen
few [fjuː] — wenig, ein paar, wenige
Good afternoon. [gʊd ˌɑːftə'nuːn] — Guten Tag. (nachmittags)
colleague ['kɒliːg] — Kollege, Kollegin
9 greet [griːt] — (be)grüßen
formally ['fɔːməlɪ] — förmlich
meet [miːt] — (sich) treffen,
    met, met — past of *meet*
phrase [freɪz] — Ausdruck, Redewendung
use [juːz] — benutzen, verwenden
introduce [ˌɪntrə'djuːs] — vorstellen, miteinander bekannt machen
missing ['mɪsɪŋ] — fehlend
near [nɪə] — bei, nahe
still [stɪl] — noch
live [lɪv] — wohnen
look after [lʊk 'ɑːftə] — betreuen
10 mailroom supervisor [ˌmeɪlruːm 'suːpəvaɪzə] — Poststellenleiter(in)
deal with ['diːl wɪð] — sich befassen mit, umgehen mit
mail [meɪl] — Post, mit der Post schicken
receptionist [rɪ'sepʃənɪst] — Herr/Dame am Empfang
secretary ['sekrətrɪ] — Sekretär(in)
clerk [klɑːk] — Büroangestellte(r), kaufmännische(r) Angestellte(r)
filing ['faɪlɪŋ] — Ablage
welcome ['welkəm] — begrüßen, empfangen
different ['dɪfrənt] — verschieden
type [taɪp] — tippen, eingeben
report [rɪ'pɔːt] — Bericht
staff [stɑːf] — Personal, Mitarbeiter
pay [peɪ] — Lohn, Gehalt
conditions [kən'dɪʃnz] — Arbeitsbedingungen
correct [kə'rekt] — berichtigen, korrigieren
11 put in order [ˌpʊt ɪn 'ɔːdə] — in richtiger Reihenfolge ordnen

	check [tʃek]	überprüfen, kontrollieren	
	fax machine ['fæks məʃi:n]	Faxgerät	
	diary ['daɪəri]	Terminkalender	
	together [tə'geðə]	zusammen	
	usually ['ju:ʒuəli]	normalerweise, gewöhnlich	
	o'clock [ə'klɒk]	volle Stunde, um ... Uhr	
	various ['veərɪəs]	verschiedene	
	stationery cupboard ['steɪʃnri ˌkʊbəd]	Schrank für Büromaterial	
	order ['ɔ:də]	bestellen	
	store [stɔ:]	Lager	
	envelope ['envələʊp]	Briefumschlag	
	three times a week ['θri: taɪmz ə wi:k]	dreimal pro Woche	
12	record card ['rekɔ:d kɑ:d]	Karteikarte	
	marketing ['mɑ:kɪtɪŋ]	Marketing	
	purchasing ['pɜ:tʃəsɪŋ]	Einkauf	
	same ['seɪm]	gleiche(r, s), der-, die, dasselbe	
	age [eɪdʒ]	Alter	
	date of birth [deɪt əv bɜ:θ]	Geburtsdatum	
	nearly ['nɪəli]	beinahe, fast	
	position [pə'zɪʃən]	Stellung, Position	

UNIT 2

14	equipment [ɪ'kwɪpmənt]	Ausstattung
	ruler ['ru:lə]	Lineal
	calculator ['kælkjuleɪtə]	Taschenrechner
	desk lamp ['desk læmp]	Schreibtischlampe
	stapler ['steɪplə]	Hefter
	staple ['steɪpl]	Heftklammer
	hole punch ['həʊl pʌntʃ]	Locher
	file [faɪl]	Aktenordner
	paper clip ['peɪpəklɪp]	Büroklammer
	notepad ['nəʊtpæd]	Notizblock
	wastepaper bin ['weɪstpeɪpə bɪn]	Papierkorb
15	corner ['kɔ:nə]	Ecke
	extension ... [ɪk'stenʃn]	Apparat ...
	know [nəʊ], knew, known	wissen
	drawer [drɔ:]	Schublade

	ground floor [ˌgraʊnd 'flɔ:]	Erdgeschoss	
16	pick up [pɪk 'ʌp]	aufheben, hochheben	
	empty ['emptɪ]	leer	
17	form [fɔ:m]	Form	
	monthly ['mʌnθli]	monatlich	
	pay cheque ['peɪ ˌtʃek]	Gehaltsscheck, -zahlung	
	early ['ɜ:lɪ]	früh	
	each [i:tʃ]	jede(r, s)	
	because [bɪ'kɒz]	weil	
18	reception [rɪ'sepʃn]	Rezeption, Empfang	
	canteen [kæn'ti:n]	Kantine	
	distribution [ˌdɪstrɪ'bju:ʃn]	Vertrieb	
	lift [lɪft]	Fahrstuhl	
	R&D (research and development) [rɪ'sɜ:tʃ ən dɪ'veləpmənt]	Forschung und Entwicklung	
	meeting room ['mi:tɪŋ ru:m]	Besprechungsraum	
	finance ['faɪnæns]	Finanzabteilung	
	M.D (managing director) [ˌmænɪdʒɪŋ də'rektə]	Geschäftsführer(in)	
	office services [ˌɒfɪs 'sɜ:vɪsɪz]	Büroservice, zentraler Dienst	
	corridor ['kɒrɪdɔ:]	Gang, Flur	
	opposite ['ɒpəzɪt]	gegenüber	
	stairs [steəz]	Treppe	
	direction [dɪ'rekʃn]	Richtung	
	next to ['nekst tə]	neben	
19	upstairs [ˌʌp'steəz]	(nach) oben	
	downstairs [ˌdaʊn'steəz]	(nach) unten	
	conversation [ˌkɒnvə'seɪʃn]	Gespräch	
	memo ['meməʊ]	Notiz, Merkzettel	
20	draw [drɔ:]	zeichnen	
	workplace ['wɜ:kpleɪs]	Arbeitsplatz	
	mark [mɑ:k]	markieren	
	important [ɪm'pɔ:tnt]	wichtig	
	prepare [prɪ'peə]	vorbereiten	
	explanation [ˌeksplə'neɪʃn]	Beschreibung	
	while [waɪl]	während	
	follow ['fɒləʊ]	folgen	
	reach [ri:tʃ]	erreichen	
	between [bɪ'twi:n]	zwischen	
21	statement ['steɪtmənt]	Aussage	
	negative ['negətɪv]	Verneinung	

Chronologisches Wörterverzeichnis

UNIT 3

22	**urgent** ['ɜːdʒənt]	dringend
	supply [sə'plaɪ]	(be)liefern
	following ['fɒləʊɪŋ]	folgend(es, er)
	goods [gʊdz]	Waren, Güter
	cat (catalogue) ['kætəlɒg]	Katalog
	detail ['diːteɪl]	Einzelheit, Detail
	steel [stiːl]	Stahl
	qty (quantity) ['kwɒntətɪ]	Menge, Quantität
	ton [tʌn]	Tonne
	unit price [juːnɪt 'praɪs]	Stückpreis
	total ['təʊtl]	Endsumme, Gesamtpreis
	value ['væljuː]	Wert
23	**emergency** [ɪ'mɜːdʒənsɪ]	Notfall
	department [dɪ'pɑːtmənt]	Abteilung
	be responsible for [biː rɪ'spɒnsəbl fɔː]	verantwortlich sein
	material [mə'tɪərɪəl]	Material, Stoff
	supplier [sə'plaɪə]	Anbieter
	make sure [ˌmeɪk 'ʃɔː]	absichern, sicherstellen
	delivery (pl -ies) [dɪ'lɪvərɪ]	(Aus)lieferung
	ago [ə'gəʊ]	vor
	due by ['djuː ˌbaɪ]	fällig
	midday [ˌmɪd'deɪ]	Mittag, mittags
	dispatch [dɪ'spætʃ]	aufgeben, wegschicken
	truck [trʌk]	Lastkraftwagen
	via ['vaɪə]	durch, über
	Channel Tunnel [ˌtʃænl 'tʌnl]	Kanaltunnel
	be in shock [ˌbiː ɪn 'ʃɒk]	schockiert sein
	casualty (pl -ies) ['kæʒʊəltɪ]	Opfer
	ferry ['ferɪ]	Fähre
	It doesn't matter. [ɪt ˌdʌznt 'mætə]	Es ist egal.
	try [traɪ]	probieren, versuchen
	expect [ɪk'spekt]	erwarten, vermuten
	be on the phone [ˌbiː ɒn ðə 'fəʊn]	telefonieren
	be lucky [biː 'lʌkɪ]	Glück haben
	book [bʊk]	buchen, bestellen
	cross [krɒs]	überqueren, durchqueren
	exact(ly) [ɪg'zækt(lɪ)]	exakt, genau
	turn [tɜːn]	(sich) drehen
	smile [smaɪl]	lächeln
24	**decide** [dɪ'saɪd]	(sich) entscheiden, sich entschließen
25	**infinitive** [ɪn'fɪnətɪv]	Grundform des Verbs
	necessary ['nesəsərɪ]	nötig, notwendig
26	**grow** [grəʊ], **grew, grown**	wachsen
	product planning [ˌprɒdʌkt 'plænɪŋ]	Produktplanung
	design [dɪ'zaɪn]	Design
	accounts [ə'kaʊnts]	Buchhaltung
	training ['treɪnɪŋ]	Ausbildungsabteilung
	organization chart [ˌɔːgənaɪ'zeɪʃn tʃɑːt]	Organisationsübersicht
	join [dʒɔɪn]	beginnen, Arbeit aufnehmen
	really ['rɪəlɪ]	wirklich, eigentlich
	figure ['fɪgə]	Zahl
	move [muːv]	wechseln
	senior accountant [ˌsiːnɪə ə'kaʊntənt]	leitende(r) Buchhalter(in)
	train [treɪn]	eine (Berufs)ausbildung machen, ausbilden
	car maker ['kɑː ˌmeɪkə]	Autohersteller
27	**customer** ['kʌstəmə]	Kunde, Kundin
	sales representative ['seɪlz reprɪˌzentətɪv]	(Handels-)Vertreter(in)
	break [breɪk] **broke, broken**	brechen, kaputtmachen
	break down [ˌbreɪk 'daʊn]	zusammenbrechen
	break out [ˌbreɪk 'aʊt]	ausbrechen
	seem [siːm]	scheinen
	control system [kən'trəʊl ˌsɪstəm]	Kontrollsystem
	crash [kræʃ]	zusammenstoßen
	back [bæk]	(Zug)ende
	crash ['kræʃ]	Zusammenstoß
	petrol tank ['petrəl tæŋk]	(Benzin)tank
	damage ['dæmɪdʒ]	Schaden
28	**note** [nəʊt]	Notiz
	branch [brɑːntʃ]	Filiale, Zweigstelle
	technical school ['teknɪkl ˌskuːl]	Gewerbeschule
	local ['ləʊkl]	örtlich
	until [ən'tɪl]	bis
	yourself [jɔː'self]	sich selbst
	expression [ɪk'spreʃn]	Ausdruck
	recently ['riːsntlɪ]	neulich, kürzlich

UNIT 4

30 **monitor** ['mɒnɪtə] — Monitor, Bildschirm
disk drive ['dɪsk draɪv] — Diskettenlaufwerk
keyboard ['ki:bɔ:d] — Tastatur
blank disk [ˌblæŋk 'dɪsk] — leere Diskette
printer ['prɪntə] — Drucker
power cable ['paʊə ˌkeɪbl] — Stromkabel
microphone ['maɪkrəfəʊn] — Mikrofon
mouse pad ['maʊs ˌpæd] — Mausunterlage, Mouse Pad
illustration [ˌɪləs'treɪʃən] — Zeichnung
user's handbook [ˌju:zəz 'hændbʊk] — Benutzerhandbuch
true [tru:] — richtig

31 **magic** ['mædʒɪk] — Zauberei
fly [flaɪ] — fliegen
range [reɪndʒ] — Sortiment
advertising leaflet ['ædvətaɪzɪŋ ˌli:flət] — Werbeprospekt
could [kʊd] — könnte
copy ['kɒpɪ] — Kopie, Zweitschrift
laugh [lɑ:f] — lachen
explain [ɪk'spleɪn] — erklären
wordprocessing ['wɜ:d ˌprəʊsesɪŋ] — Textverarbeitung
copy ['kɒpɪ] — kopieren, abschreiben
keep [ki:p] — behalten
delete [dɪ'li:t] — löschen
key in ['ki: ˌɪn] — eingeben, einfügen
on-screen [ˌɒn 'skri:n] — direkt am Bildschirm
fit [fɪt] — passen
space [speɪs] — Leerraum
be able [ˌbi: 'eɪbl] — können
press [pres] — drücken
print out [prɪnt] — (aus)drucken
fantastic [fæn'tæstɪk] — fantastisch
set [set] — einstellen
real [rɪəl] — echt
study ['stʌdɪ] — Arbeitszimmer
special ['speʃl] — besondere(r,s), Sonder-
feature ['fi:tʃə] — Merkmal, Kennzeichen

32 **spare part** [ˌspeə 'pɑ:t] — Ersatzteil
item ['aɪtəm] — Artikel

33 **auto(matic)** [ˌɔ:tə'mætɪk] — automatisch
go dead [gəʊ 'ded] went, gone — ausfallen
day off [ˌdeɪ 'ɒf] — freier Tag

rep (representative) [ˌreprɪ'zentətɪv] — (Handels-)Vertreter(in)
allow [ə'laʊ] — erlauben, gestatten
ill [ɪl] — krank
Great! [greɪt] — Großartig!
cook [kʊk] — kochen
heavy ['hevɪ] — schwer
myself [maɪ'self] — selbst
coffee maker [kɒfi meɪkə] — Kaffeemaschine

34 **tray** [treɪ] — Ablage(korb)
blind [blaɪnd] — Rollo, Jalousie
compare [kəm'peə] — vergleichen
difference ['dɪfrəns] — Unterschied
(un)labelled ['leɪbld] — (nicht) beschriftet
(un)tidy [ʌn'taɪdɪ] — (un)ordentlich, (un)aufgeräumt

35 **menu** ['menju:] — Menü
click [klɪk] — klicken
fresh line [freʃ laɪn] — neue Zeile
lose [lu:z] — verlieren
select [sə'lekt] — auswählen
capital letters [ˌkæpɪtl 'letəz] — Großbuchstaben

36 **plan** [plæn] — planen, vorhaben
brochure ['brəʊʃə] — Broschüre, Prospekt
shelf [ʃelf] — Aufsatz
sliding shelf [slaɪdɪŋ ʃelf] — Auszug
available [ə'veɪləbl] — erhältlich, verfügbar
grey [greɪ] — grau
size [saɪz] — Maße

UNIT 5

38 **appointment** [ə'pɔɪntmənt] — Termin
discuss [dɪ'skʌs] — besprechen
tool [tu:l] — Werkzeug
interview ['ɪntəvju:] — Vorstellungsgespräch

39 **usual** ['ju:ʒl] — gewöhnlich
free [fri:] — frei
meeting ['mi:tɪŋ] — Besprechung, Sitzung
show round [ˌʃəʊ 'raʊnd] — herumführen
favour ['feɪvə] — Gefallen
of course [əv 'kɔ:s] — natürlich, selbstverständlich
firm [fɜ:m] — Firma
journey ['dʒɜ:nɪ] — Reise, Fahrt

Chronologisches Wörterverzeichnis

	you're welcome [jɔː 'welkəm]	nichts zu danken, keine Ursache
	would you like ... [ˌwʊd juː 'laɪk]	möchten Sie ...
	sugar ['ʃʊɡə]	Zucker
	taste [teɪst]	schmecken
40	happen ['hæpən]	passieren, geschehen
	meaning ['miːnɪŋ]	Bedeutung, Sinn
	suggest [sə'dʒest]	vorschlagen
	choose [tʃuːz]	wählen, aussuchen
	bicycle ['baɪsɪkl]	Fahrrad
	ship [ʃɪp]	Schiff
	air ['eə]	Luft
	rail [reɪl]	Zug
	sea [siː]	Meer
41	take a seat [ˌteɪk ə 'siːt]	Platz nehmen
	caller ['kɔːlə]	Anrufer
	repeat [rɪ'piːt]	wiederholen
	maternity leave [mə'tɜːnəti ˌliːv]	Mutterschaftsurlaub
	change [tʃeɪndʒ]	umwandeln
43	manufacturing [ˌmænju'fæktʃərɪŋ]	Herstellung, Produktion
	operation [ˌɒpə'reɪʃn]	Filiale
	anywhere ['enɪweə]	irgendwo
44	act [ækt]	vorspielen

UNIT 6

48	remember [rɪ'membə]	sich erinnern
	title ['taɪtl]	Bezeichnung
49	contact ['kɒntækt]	Kontakt
	hard-working [ˌhɑːd 'wɜːkɪŋ]	fleißig
	useful ['juːsfl]	nützlich
	field [fiːld]	Bereich, Gebiet
	experience [ɪk'spɪərɪəns]	Erfahrung
	conference [kɒnfərəns]	Konferenz
	worry ['wʌri]	sich Sorgen machen
	section ['sekʃn]	Abteilung
	hope [həʊp]	hoffen
	enjoy [ɪn'dʒɔɪ]	gefallen
	probably ['prɒbəbli]	wahrscheinlich
50	actually ['æktʃʊli]	eigentlich, wirklich
	successful [sək'sesfl]	erfolgreich
51	certainly ['sɜːtnli]	sicherlich, gewiss
	shower ['ʃaʊə]	Dusche
	rest [rest]	Pause
	snack [snæk]	Imbiss
	meal [miːl]	Essen
	tired ['taɪəd]	müde
	accept [ək'sept]	annehmen, akzeptieren
	photocopier ['fəʊtəʊkɒpɪ]	Fotokopierer
	hit [hɪt]	schlagen
	repair [rɪ'peə]	reparieren
	advert ['ædvɜːt]	Anzeige, Inserat
	application letter [ˌæplɪ'keɪʃn ˌletə]	Bewerbungsbrief, -schreiben
	spelling mistake ['spelɪŋ mɪˌsteɪk]	(Recht)schreibfehler
52	instruction [ɪn'strʌkʃn]	Anweisung
	disconnect [ˌdɪskə'nekt]	ausschalten, abstellen
	cover ['kʌvə]	zudecken, abdecken
	in case of lightning ['laɪtnɪŋ]	bei Blitzgefahr
	enough [ɪ'nʌf]	ausreichend, genug
	heater ['hiːtə]	Heizgerät
	market ['mɑːkɪt]	Markt
	pie chart ['paɪ ˌtʃɑːt]	Kreisdiagramm
	three quarters [ˌθriː 'kwɔːtəz]	drei Viertel
	two thirds [ˌtuː 'θɜːdz]	zwei Drittel
	half [hɑːf]	Hälfte
	third [θɜːd]	Drittel
	quarter ['kwɔːtə]	Viertel
	eighth [eɪtθ]	Achtel
	abroad [ə'brɔːd]	im Ausland, ins Ausland
53	recent ['riːsnt]	letzte(r,s)
	graph [grɑːf]	Diagramm
	table ['teɪbl]	Tabelle
	rise [raɪz] rose, risen	steigen, wachsen
	remain [rɪ'meɪn]	bleiben
	rapidly ['ræpɪdli]	schnell
54	basic skills [ˌbeɪsɪk 'skɪlz]	Grundfertigkeiten
	flexible ['fleksəbl]	flexibel
	office administration [ˌɒfɪs ədmɪnɪ'streɪʃn]	Büroorganisation
	book-keeping ['bʊkiːpɪŋ]	Buchhaltung
	course [kɔːs]	Kurs, Lehrgang
	economics [iːkə'nɒmɪks]	Betriebswirtschaft
	mean [miːn]	bedeuten
	pretty ['prɪti]	ziemlich, ganz
	specialist ['speʃəlɪst]	Spezialist(in)

55	accountant [əˈkaʊntənt]	Buchhalter(in)		62	offering help [ˌɒfərɪŋ ˈhelp]	Hilfe anbieten
	clerical worker [ˈklerɪkl ˌwɜːkə]	Schreib-, Bürokraft			take/leave a message [ˌteɪk/ˌliːv ə ˈmesɪdʒ]	etwas ausrichten / Nachricht hinterlassen
	programmer [ˈprəʊgræmə]	Programmierer(in)		63	die [daɪ]	sterben
	agree [əˈgriː]	übereinstimmen, zustimmen			lie [laɪ]	liegen
					belong [bɪˈlɒŋ]	gehören
					hate [heɪt]	hassen
					wish [wɪʃ]	wünschen
					believe [bɪˈliːv]	glauben

UNIT 7

UNIT 8

56	flat [flæt]	Wohnung
	dishwasher [ˈdɪʃwɒʃə]	Geschirrspülmaschine
	video recorder [ˈvɪdiəʊ rɪˌkɔːdə]	Videorecorder
	washing machine [ˈwɒʃɪŋ məˌʃiːn]	Waschmaschine
	afford [əˈfɔːd]	sich leisten
	survey [ˈsɜːveɪ]	Umfrage
	choice [tʃɔɪs]	Auswahl, ausgewählter Artikel
57	phone call [ˈfəʊn kɔːl]	Anruf
	alone [əˈləʊn]	allein
	spell [spel]	buchstabieren
	double [ˈdʌbl]	doppelt
	bankrupt [ˈbæŋkrʌpt]	bankrott
	terrible [ˈterəbl]	schrecklich, fürchterlich
	reference number [ˈrefrəns ˌnʌmbə]	Aktenzeichen, Kennziffer
	valid [ˈvælɪd]	gültig
	stock list [ˈstɒk ˌlɪst]	Warenliste
	call up [ˈkɔːl ˌʌp]	aufrufen
	finally [ˈfaɪnəli]	schließlich
	shout [ʃaʊt]	rufen
	promise [ˈprɒmɪs]	versprechen
58	go out of business [ˌgəʊ aʊt ɒv ˈbɪznəs]	in Konkurs gehen
	passport [ˈpɑːspɔːt]	Reisepass
	agency [ˈeɪdʒənsi]	Vertretung
	contract [ˈkɒntrækt]	Vertrag
59	agent [ˈeɪdʒənt]	Vertreter
	shopping [ˈʃɒpɪŋ]	Einkauf
	future [ˈfjuːtʃə]	Zukunft
61	pick up (telephone) [ˌpɪk ˈʌp]	abnehmen
	dictate [dɪkˈteɪt]	diktieren
	abbreviation [əˌbriːviˈeɪʃn]	Abkürzung
	airline [ˈeəlaɪn]	Luftfahrtgesellschaft
	spelling code [ˈspelɪŋ ˌkəʊd]	Buchstabiercode

64	manufacturer [ˌmænjʊˈfæktʃərə]	Hersteller
	complex [ˈkɒmpleks]	kompliziert
	freight forwarding agency [ˈfreɪt ˌfɔːwədɪŋ ˈeɪdʒənsi]	Güterspedition
	iron ore [ˌaɪən ˈɔː]	Eisenerz
	steelworks [ˈstiːlwɜːks]	Stahlwerk
	hot-house rose [ˌhɒthaʊs ˈrəʊz]	Treibhausrose
	secret [ˈsiːkrɪt]	geheim
	courier [ˈkʊrɪə]	Kurier
	van [væn]	Lieferwagen, Transporter
65	schedule [ˈʃedjuːl]	Zeitplan
	handle [ˈhændl]	erledigen, bearbeiten
	include [ɪnˈkluːd]	einschließen
	shipment [ˈʃɪpmənt]	Verschiffung
	suppose [səˈpəʊz]	glauben, annehmen
	method [ˈmeθəd]	Methode, Verfahren
	route [ruːt]	Route, Strecke
	coast [kəʊst]	Küste
	lunchtime [ˈlʌntʃtaɪm]	Mittagszeit
66	arrangement [əˈreɪndʒmənt]	Absprache, Vorbereitung
	comparative [kəmˈpærətɪv]	Steigerungsform des Adjektivs
	less [les]	weniger
	practical [ˈpræktɪkl]	praktisch, realistisch
	comfortable [ˈkʌmftəbl]	bequem
	cheap [tʃiːp]	billig, günstig
	superlative [suˈpɜːlətɪv]	höchste Steigerungsform des Adjektivs
	least [liːst]	wenigste(r, s), geringste(r, s)
67	reliable [rɪˈlaɪəbl]	zuverlässig
	loud [laʊd]	laut
	turn down [ˌtɜːn ˈdaʊn]	leiser stellen

Chronologisches Wörterverzeichnis

	paragraph ['pærəgrɑ:f]	Absatz, Abschnitt
	bracket ['brækɪt]	Klammer
	immediate [ɪ'mi:dɪət]	sofort, umgehend
	load [ləʊd]	beladen
	document ['dɒkjʊmənt]	Frachtpapier(e)
	careful ['keəfl]	sorgfältig
	motorway ['məʊtəweɪ]	Autobahn
	towards [tə'wɔ:dz]	auf … zu, in Richtung
	roadworks ['rəʊdwɜ:ks]	Straßenbauarbeiten
	slow down [sləʊ 'daʊn]	aufhalten
	south [saʊθ]	nach Süden, südlich
	traffic ['træfɪk]	Verkehr
	final ['faɪnl]	endgültig
68	weigh [weɪ]	wiegen
	express delivery company [ɪk,spres dɪ'lɪvrɪ ,kʌmpəni]	Expresslieferant, Kourierdienst
	collection [kə'lekʃn]	Abholung
	length [leŋθ]	Länge
	package ['pækɪdʒ]	Paket
69	engaged [ɪn'geɪdʒd]	besetzt
	hold (the line) [,həʊld (ðə 'laɪn)]	bleiben (am Apparat)
	rather ['rɑ:ðə]	ziemlich, ganz
	sign [saɪn]	unterschreiben
71	worse, worst [wɜ:s, wɜ:st]	schlechter, am schlechtesten

UNIT 9

72	surprise [sə'praɪz]	Überraschung
	return [rɪ'tɜ:n]	Rückkehr
	arrange [ə'reɪndʒ]	arrangieren
	return [rɪ'tɜ:n]	zurückkehren
	previously ['pri:vɪəslɪ]	vorher
73	yet [jet]	schon, bereits
	airport ['eəpɔ:t]	Flughafen
	nobody ['nəʊbədi]	niemand
	trip (back) [trɪp (bæk)]	(Rück-)reise, -fahrt
74	give back [,gɪv 'bæk] gave, given	zurückgeben
	pack [pæk]	packen
	present ['preznt]	Geschenk
75	spend [spend] spent, spent	ausgeben
	switch [swɪtʃ]	Schalter
76	concert ['kɒnsət]	Konzert
77	member ['membə]	Mitglied
	single ticket ['sɪŋgl]	einfache Fahrkarte
	passenger ['pæsɪndʒə]	Passagier, Fluggast
78	terminal ['tɜ:mɪnl]	Endstation

UNIT 10

80	suitcase ['su:tkeɪs]	Koffer
	exchange bureau [ɪks'tʃeɪndʒ ,bjʊərəʊ]	Wechselstelle, Wechselstube
	luggage ['lʌgɪdʒ]	Gepäck
81	guys (AE) [gaɪz]	Leute (umgangssprachlich)
	autumn ['ɔ:təm]	Herbst
	produce [prə'dju:s]	produzieren, herstellen
	amazing [ə'meɪzɪŋ]	erstaunlich
	sound [saʊnd]	klingen
	map [mæp]	Wegskizze, Stadtplan
	good luck [,gʊd 'lʌk]	Viel Glück
82	far [fɑ:]	weit
	on foot [ɒn fʊt]	zu Fuß
	situation [sɪtʃʊ'eɪʃn]	Situation
	result [rɪ'zʌlt]	Ergebnis
	arm [ɑ:m]	Arm
83	land [lænd]	landen
	mend [mend]	reparieren
	motorbike ['məʊtəbaɪk]	Motorrad
	girlfriend ['gɜ:lfrend]	Freundin
	theatre ['θɪətə]	Theater
84	reservation [,rezə'veɪʃn]	Reservierung
	taxi-rank ['tæksi ,ræŋk]	Taxistand
	straight ahead [,streɪt'hed]	geradeaus
	since [sɪns]	seit
85	invite [ɪn'vaɪt]	einladen
86	during ['djʊərɪŋ]	während

UNIT 11

90	describe [dɪ'skraɪb]	beschreiben
91	responsibility (pl -ies) [rɪ,spɒnsəbɪlətɪ]	Tätigkeit, Verantwortlichkeit
	outside ['aʊtsaɪd]	außerhalb
	warehouse ['weəhaʊs]	Lager
	ring [rɪŋ] rang, rung	läuten, klingeln
	matter ['mætə]	Angelegenheit
	traditional [trə'dɪʃnəl]	traditionell
	sightseeing ['saɪtsi:ɪŋ]	Besichtigung, Stadtbesichtigung
	it's worth [ɪts 'wɜ:θ]	wert sein, sich lohnen
92	industry (pl -ies) ['ɪndəstrɪ]	Industrie
	salary ['sælərɪ]	Gehalt
93	manage ['mænɪdʒ]	schaffen
	mind [maɪnd]	jdm. etwas ausmachen

risk [rɪsk]	riskieren	
jog [dʒɒg]	joggen	
ski [skiː]	Ski laufen	
waste of time [ˌweɪst əv 'taɪm]	Zeitverschwendung	
paperwork ['peɪpəwɜːk]	Schreibarbeit	
exam [ɪg'zæm]	Prüfung	
no point in … ['nəʊ ˌpɔɪnt ɪn]	keinen Zweck haben	
94 railway ['reɪlweɪ]	Eisenbahn	
bridge [brɪdʒ]	Brücke	
traffic lights ['træfɪk ˌlaɪts]	Ampel	
church [tʃɜːtʃ]	Kirche	
sports centre ['spɔːts ˌsentə]	Sportzentrum	
tourist information office [ˌtʊərɪst ɪnfə'meɪʃn 'ɒfɪs]	Touristeninformationsbüro	
bookshop ['bʊkʃɒp]	Buchhandlung	
95 area ['eərɪə]	Gegend	
chemist's ['kemɪsts]	Drogerie, Apotheke	
credit control ['kredɪt kənˌtrəʊl]	Kreditabteilung	
96 organize ['ɔːgənaɪz]	organisieren	
dislike [dɪs'laɪk]	nicht mögen	
herself [hɜː'self]	sie selbst	
himself [hɪm'self]	er selbst	

UNIT 12

98	tour [tʊə]	Tour, Rundfahrt
	stop [stɒp]	Aufenthalt, Zwischenlandung
99	Far East [ˌfɑː 'iːst]	Ferner Osten
	regards [rɪ'gɑːdz]	Gruß
100	take [teɪk]	dauern
	though [ðəʊ]	doch, tatsächlich
101	depart [dɪ'pɑːt]	abfliegen
102	advise [əd'vaɪz]	verständigen, Bescheid geben
104	suggestion [sə'dʒestʃən]	Vorschlag
	suit [suːt]	passen

UNIT 13

106	complaint [kəm'pleɪnt]	Reklamation
	capital city (pl -ies) [ˌkæpɪtl 'sɪti]	Hauptstadt
107	light unit ['laɪt ˌjuːnɪt]	Lampe, Leuchte

standard ['stændəd]	Norm	
container [kən'teɪnə]	Behälter, Container	
at sb's expense [ɪk'spens]	auf Kosten, zu Lasten von	
engineer [ˌendʒɪ'nɪə]	Techniker(in)	
excellent ['eksələnt]	ausgezeichnet, hervorragend	
air fare ['eəˌfeə]	Flugpreis	
108 impossible [ɪm'pɒsəbl]	unmöglich, undenkbar	
solve [sɒlv]	lösen	
pass (an exam) [pɑːs]	bestehen	
none [nʌn]	keine (r, s)	
regret [rɪ'gret]	bedauern	
inform [ɪn'fɔːm]	informieren, benachrichtigen	
unsatisfactory [ˌʌnsætɪs'fæktri]	unbefriedigend, nicht zufriedenstellend	
style [staɪl]	Schnitt, Art	
in fact [ɪn 'fækt]	tatsächlich, eigentlich	
109 properly ['prɒpəli]	richtig, korrekt	
110 clock [klɒk]	Uhr	
etc. [ˌet'setrə]	usw.	
scratched [skrætʃ]	zerkratzt	
cracked [kræk]	gesprungen	
bent [bent]	verbogen	
description [dɪ'skrɪpʃn]	Beschreibung	
comment ['kɒment]	Bemerkung, Kommentar	
111 diagram ['daɪəgræm]	grafische Darstellung, Diagramm	
stock level ['stɒk ˌlevl]	Warenbestand	
raw materials [ˌrɔː mə'tɪərɪəlz]	Rohstoffe	
shipping document ['ʃɪpɪŋ ˌdɒkjument]	Frachtpapiere	
112 case [keɪs]	Box	
solar cell ['səʊlə sel]	Solarzelle	

UNIT 14

114	build [bɪld]	bauen
	beauty spot ['bjuːti ˌspɒt]	hübsches/schönes Fleckchen (Erde)
	public [ˌpʌblɪk]	öffentlich
	agenda [ə'dʒendə]	Tagesordnung
	discussion [dɪ'skʌʃn]	Diskussion
	community [kə'mjuːnəti]	Gemeinde
	fight [faɪt]	(be)kämpfen
	government ['gʌvənmənt]	Regierung

Chronologisches Wörterverzeichnis

clear [klɪər]	klar	
plan of action [ˌplæn ɒv 'ækʃn]	Plan	
poster ['pəʊstə]	Plakat	
advertise ['ædvətaɪz]	bekannt machen	
reason ['riːzn]	Grund	
flip chart ['flɪp tʃɑːt]	Flip-chart	
white board ['waɪt bɔːd]	White Board	
overhead projector [ˌəʊvəhed prə'dʒektə]	Tageslichtprojektor, Overheadprojektor	
loudspeaker [ˌlaʊd'spiːkə]	Lautsprecher	
video camera ['vɪdiəʊ ˌkæmrə]	Videokamera	
cassette recorder [kə'set rɪˌkɔːdə]	Kassettenrekorder	
slide projector ['slaɪd prəˌdʒektə]	Diaprojektor	

115 **presentation** [ˌprezn'teɪʃn] — Vorführung, Präsentation
facility [fə'sɪlɪti] — Einrichtung, Möglichkeit
translator [træns'leɪtə] — Übersetzer(in)
interpreter [ɪn'tɜːprɪtə] — Dolmetscher(in)
slot [slɒt] — (Programm)abschnitt
especially [ɪ'speʃəli] — besonders
classroom ['klɑːsruːm] — Klassenraum
116 **communicate** [kə'mjuːnɪkeɪt] — sich verständigen, kommunizieren
117 **complain** [kəm'pleɪn] — sich beklagen, beschweren
rewrite [ˌriː'raɪt] — umschreiben
polite [pə'laɪt] — höflich
lend [lend] — leihen
wide [waɪd] — breit
narrow ['nærəʊ] — schmal
low [ləʊ] — niedrig
118 **attend** [ə'tend] — teilnehmen an
neither ['naɪðə] — keine
119 **ideal** [aɪ'dɪəl] — ideal
view [vjuː] — Blick, Ausblick
club [klʌb] — Club
marine [mə'riːn] — Meeres-
twin-bed [ˌtwɪn'bed] — Zweibett-
against [ə'genst] — gegen
120 **vegetarian** [ˌvedʒə'teəriən] — Vegetarier(in)
participant [pɑː'tɪsɪpənt] — Teilnehmer(in)

UNIT 15

123 **celebrate** ['selɪbreɪt] — feiern
project ['prɒdʒekt] — Projekt
head of the table [ˌhed əv ðə 'teɪbl] — Stirnseite des Tisches
ladies and gentlemen ['leɪdɪz ən 'dʒentlmən] — Meine Damen und Herren (Anrede)
step [step] — Schritt
develop [dɪ'veləp] — entwickeln
talent ['tælənt] — Talent, Begabung
meat dish ['miːt ˌdɪʃ] — Fleischgericht
veal [viːl] — Kalbfleisch
tasty ['teɪsti] — schmackhaft
pork [pɔːk] — Schweinefleisch
dumpling ['dʌmplɪŋ] — Kloß, Knödel
filling ['fɪlɪŋ] — sättigend
124 **recommend** [ˌrekə'mend] — empfehlen
starter ['stɑːtə] — Vorspeise
mushroom ['mʌʃrʊm] — Champignon
bake [beɪk] — backen
oven ['ʌvn] — Backofen
wine [waɪn] — Wein
raise [reɪz] — erheben
tomato (pl -es) [tə'mɑːtəʊ] — Tomate
soup [suːp] — Suppe
tiring ['taɪrɪŋ] — anstrengend, ermüdend
125 **guess** [ges] — glauben, annehmen
clause [klɔːz] — Satzteil
rich [rɪtʃ] — ergiebig
talented ['tæləntɪd] — begabt, talentiert
126 **progress** ['prəʊgres] — Fortschritt
reporter [rɪ'pɔːtə] — Reporter(in)
link [lɪŋk] — Verbindung
infrastructure ['ɪnfrəstrʌktʃə] — Infrastruktur
consider [kən'sɪdə] — in Erwägung ziehen, nachdenken über
last [lɑːst] — (an)dauern
127 **casserole** ['kæsərəʊl] — geschmortes Fleischgericht, Gulasch
popular ['pɒpjʊlə] — beliebt
role [rəʊl] — Rolle
128 **subject** ['sʌbdʒɪkt] — Thema, Fachgebiet
tick [tɪk] — abhaken
salesperson ['seɪlzpɜːsn] — Verkäufer(in)

CORRESPONDENCE A

132 **general** [ˌdʒenrəl] — allgemein
enquiry [ɪn'kwaɪri] — Anfrage
information [ˌɪnfə'meɪʃn] — Auskunft, Information
sewing machine ['səʊɪŋ məˌʃiːn] — Nähmaschine
for the attention of [fɔː ði: ə'tenʃn ɒv] — zu Händen von
receive [rɪ'siːv] — erhalten, bekommen
Chamber of Commerce [ˌtʃeɪmbə əv 'kɒmɜːs] — Handelskammer
current ['kʌrənt] — aktuell, letzte(r, s)
price list [praɪs lɪst] — Preisliste
industrial [ɪn'dʌstrɪəl] — Industrie-
look forward to [lʊk 'fɔːwəd tə] — sich freuen auf
as soon as possible [æz ˌsuːn əz 'pɒsəbl] — so schnell wie möglich
yours faithfully [jɔːz 'feɪθfəli] — Hochachtungsvoll, Mit freundlichen Grüßen

133 **addressed** [ə'drest] — adressiert, gerichtet an
pass [pɑːs] — weiterleiten
interested in ['ɪntrəstɪd ɪn] — interessiert
comprehensive [kɒmprɪ'hensɪv] — Gesamt-
letterhead ['letəhed] — Briefkopf

134 **specific** [spə'sɪfɪk] — speziell
quotation [kwəʊ'teɪʃn] — Kostenvoranschlag
grateful ['greɪtfl] — dankbar
computerized [kəm'pjuːtəraɪzd] — Computer-
button-hole ['bʌtnhəʊl] — Knopfloch
software pack ['sɒfweə ˌpæk] — Softwarepaket
price [praɪs] — Preis
quote [kwəʊt] — nennen, angeben
DDP (Delivered Duty Paid) [dɪˌlɪvəd ˌdjuːti 'peɪd] — Geliefert verzollt
term [tɜːm] — Bedingung
prompt [prɒmpt] — sofort, prompt
reply [rɪ'plaɪ] — Antwort
modernize ['mɒdənaɪz] — modernisieren
yours sincerely [jɔːz sɪn'sɪəli] — Mit freundlichen Grüßen
kind [kaɪnd] — Art, Sorte

135 **offer** ['ɒfə] — Angebot
require [rɪ'kwaɪə] — benötigen
as requested [æz rɪ'kwestɪd] — wie gewünscht
willing ['wɪlɪŋ] — gewillt sein
offer ['ɒfə] — anbieten
further ['fɜːðə] — weitere(s, r)
cash [kæʃ] — Barzahlung
discount ['dɪskaʊnt] — Rabatt, Skonto
payment ['peɪmənt] — Bezahlung
within [wɪðɪn] — innerhalb
exception [ɪk'sepʃn] — Ausnahme
consignment [kən'saɪnmənt] — Sendung
immediately [ɪ'miːdiətli] — sofort, umgehend
on receipt [ɒn rɪ'siːt] — nach Erhalt
remaining [rɪ'meɪnɪŋ] — übrig, restlich
delighted [dɪ'laɪtɪd] — sehr erfreut

136 **dated** [deɪtɪd] — datiert
idea [aɪ'dɪə] — Vorstellung
deliver [dɪ'lɪvə] — liefern
cost [kɒst] — Kosten
seller ['selə] — Verkäufer(in)
buyer ['baɪə] — Käufer(in), Einkäufer(in)
lower ['ləʊə] — niedriger
such [sʌtʃ] — solche(r,s)

137 **satisfied** ['sætɪsfaɪd] — zufrieden
high quality [ˌhaɪ 'kwɒləti] — Qualitäts-
less [les] — abzüglich

138 **against** [ə'genst] — gegenüber
per cent [pə'sent] — Prozent
submit [səb'mɪt] — unterbreiten

Chronologisches Wörterverzeichnis

CORRESPONDENCE B

139	**layout** ['leɪaʊt]	Layout
	inside address [ɪnˌsaɪd ə'dres]	Anschrift des Empfängers
	salutation [ˌsælju'teɪʃn]	Anrede
	subject line ['sʌbdʒekt laɪn]	Betreff
	rare [reə]	selten
	make [meɪk]	(Marken)produkt, Marke
	original [ə'rɪdʒənl]	original
	specially ['speʃli]	speziell, extra
	manufactured [ˌmænjʊ'fæktʃəd]	hergestellt, angefertigt
	according to [ə'kɔːdɪŋ tuː]	nach
	drawing ['drɔːɪŋ]	Zeichnung
	enclose [ɪn'kləʊz]	beilegen
	complimentary close [kɒmplɪˌmentri 'kləʊz]	Schlussformel, Gruß
	signature block ['sɪgnətʃə ˌblɒk]	Unterschriftsabschnitt
	enclosure (enc.) [ɪn'kləʊzə]	Anlage
140	**run out of** ['rʌn ˌaʊt ɒv]	ausgehen, alle werden
	punctuation [ˌpʌŋktʃu'eɪʃn]	Zeichensetzung, Interpunktion
	registered [redʒɪstəd]	eingetragen, eingeschrieben
	VAT (Value Added Tax) [ˌviː eɪ 'tiː]	Mehrwertsteuer
	county (BE) ['kaʊnti]	Grafschaft
	ZIP code (AE) ['zɪp kəʊd]	Postleitzahl
	separate ['seprət]	getrennt
	comma ['kɒmə]	Komma
	initials [ɪnɪʃlz]	Initialen, Anfangsbuchstaben
141	**whether** ['weðə]	ob
	married ['mærɪd]	verheiratet
	instead of [ɪn'sted ɒv]	anstatt
	directly [də'rektli]	direkt
142	**lane** [leɪn]	Straße
	convenient [kən'viːnɪənt]	passend, günstig
143	**build up** ['bɪld ˌʌp]	aufbauen
	built, built	
	relationship [rɪ'leɪʃnʃɪp]	Beziehung
	engine ['endʒɪn]	Motor
	notification [ˌnəʊtɪfɪkeɪʃn]	Benachrichtigung
	haulage contractor ['hɔːlɪdʒ kən'træktə]	Spedition, Transportunternehmen
	couple ['kʌpl]	einige, ein paar
	keep to [kiːp tuː]	einhalten
	sheet [ʃiːt]	Seite, Blatt
144	**introduction** [ˌɪntrə'dʌkʃn]	Einleitung, Einführung
	fill in [fɪl 'ɪn]	ausfüllen
	lorry ['lɒri]	Lastwagen, LKW
	identical [aɪ'dentɪkl]	identisch
	transmit [trænz'mɪt]	übertragen
	formal ['fɔːml]	formell, förmlich
	handwritten [ˌhænd'rɪtn]	handgeschrieben
	spoken ['spəʊkn]	gesprochen
	greeting ['griːtɪŋ]	Gruß(formel)
	simply ['sɪmpli]	einfach
145	**confirmation** [ˌkɒnfə'meɪʃn]	Bestätigung
	undamaged [ˌʌn'dæmɪdʒd]	unbeschädigt
146	**leading** ['liːdɪŋ]	führend
	retailer ['riːteɪlə]	Einzelhändler(in)
	indication [ˌɪndɪ'keɪʃn]	Angabe
	trouble ['trʌbl]	Mühe
	British Consulate General [ˌbrɪtɪʃ ˌkɒnsjʊlət 'dʒenrl]	Britisches Generalkonsulat
	fleet [fliːt]	Fuhrpark
	equip [ɪ'kwɪp]	ausrüsten, ausstatten
	improve [ɪm'pruːv]	verbessern
	communication [kəˌmjuːnɪ'keɪʃn]	Verständigung
147	**have pleasure in** [hæv 'pleʒə ɪn]	sich freuen
	hesitate ['hezɪteɪt]	zögern
	mention ['menʃn]	erwähnen
	apply [ə'plaɪ]	gelten
148	**acknowledgement** [ək'nɒlɪdʒmənt]	(Empfangs)Bestätigung
	shortly ['ʃɔːtli]	in Kürze
	except (for) [ɪk'sept fə]	außer
	obvious ['ɒbvɪəs]	offensichtlich
	contain [kən'teɪn]	enthalten
	acknowledge [ək'nɒlɪdʒ]	bestätigen
	on departure [ɒn dɪ'pɑːtʃə]	bei Abfahrt

CORRESPONDENCE C

149 **helpful** ['helpfl] — hilfreich
aggressive [ə'gresɪv] — aggressiv
wholesaler ['həʊleɪlə] — Großhändler(in)
unfortunately [ʌn'fɔːtʃənɪtlɪ] — leider
although [ɔːl'ðəʊ] — obwohl
150 **worried** ['wʌrɪd] — besorgt, beunruhigt
get in touch with [get ɪn 'tʌtʃ wɪð] — in Verbindung setzen
assure [ə'ʃɔː] — versichern, zusichern
definitely ['defɪnətlɪ] — bestimmt, sicher, genau
glad [glæd] — froh
indeed [ɪn'diːd] — tatsächlich
badly ['bædlɪ] — sehr
hold up ['həʊld ʌp] — aufhalten
held, held
delay [dɪ'leɪ] — Verspätung
flooding ['flʌdɪŋ] — Überschwemmung
mechanical [mɪ'kænɪkl] — mechanisch, technisch
however [haʊ'evə] — jedoch, doch
151 **incomplete** [,ɪnkəm'pliːt] — unvollständig
zip-fastener ['zɪp,fɑːsnə] — Reißverschluss
button ['bʌtn] — Knopf
plastic ['plæstɪk] — Plastik
oversight ['əʊvəsaɪt] — Versehen
packaging department ['pækɪdʒɪŋ dɪ,pɑːtmənt] — Verpackungsabteilung
inspection [ɪn'spekʃn] — Kontrolle
procedure [prə'siːdʒə] — Verfahren
transport ['trænspɔːt] — transportieren
152 **reminder** [rɪ'maɪndə] — Mahnung
invoice ['ɪnvɔɪs] — Rechnung
friendly ['frendlɪ] — freundlich
assume [ə'sjuːm] — annehmen
either ... or ['aɪðə, ɔː] — entweder ... oder
mislay [,mɪs'leɪ] — verlegen
mislaid, mislaid
payable ['peɪəbl] — zahlbar
calculate ['kælkjʊleɪt] — kalkulieren, berechnen
basis ['beɪsɪs] — Basis, Grundlage
overdue [,əʊvə'djuː] — überfällig
outstanding [,aʊt'stændɪŋ] — ausstehend
amount [ə'maʊnt] — Summe, Betrag
in the meantime [ɪn ðə 'miːntaɪm] — in der Zwischenzeit
ignore [ɪg'nɔː] — ignorieren

153 **tough** [tʌf] — hart
competition [,kɒmpə'tɪʃn] — Konkurrenz
settle ['setl] — begleichen
price war ['praɪs wɔː] — Preiskrieg
retail ['riːteɪl] — Einzelhandel
cause [kɔːz] — verursachen
fall through the floor [,fɔːl θruː ðə 'flɔː] — in den Keller fallen
not possibly [nɒt 'pɒsəblɪ] — unmöglich
therefore ['ðeəfɔː] — deshalb
instalment [ɪn'stɔːlmənt] — Rate
effect [ɪ'fekt] — Wirkung, Auswirkung
154 **extremely** [ɪk'striːmlɪ] — sehr
dissatisfied [,dɪs'sætɪsfaɪd] — unzufrieden
improvement [ɪm'pruːvmənt] — Verbesserung
breakdown ['breɪkdaʊn] — Panne
modem ['məʊdem] — Modem
155 **component** [kəm'pəʊnənt] — Bauelement, Einzelteil
apologise [ə'pɒlədʒaɪz] — sich entschuldigen
forward ['fɔːwəd] — liefern, nachsenden
fashion belt ['fæʃn ,belt] — (modischer) Gürtel
coloured ['kʌləd] — farbig
156 **overlook** [,əʊvə'lʊk] — übersehen
recession [rɪ'seʃn] — Rezession
serious ['sɪərɪəs] — ernst
financial [faɪ'nænʃl] — finanziell, wirtschaftlich
model letter ['mɒdl ,letə] — Beispielbrief
cheque [tʃek] — Scheck
157 **luxury** ['lʌkʃərɪ] — Luxus-
suffer ['sʌfə] — leiden
particularly [pə'tɪkjʊləlɪ] — besonders
place [pleɪs] — erteilen
lead [liːd] — führen
led, led
drop [drɒp] — Rückgang

Alphabetisches Wörterverzeichnis

Dieses Wörterverzeichnis enthält in alphabetischer Reihenfolge alle Wörter, die im Buch auftreten.
Die Zahl nach dem Stichwort bezieht sich auf die Seite, auf der das Wort zum ersten Mal erscheint.
AE = amerikanisches Englisch; BE = britisches Englisch

A

abbreviation 61	Abkürzung
able, be ~ 31	können
abroad 52	im Ausland, ins Ausland
accept 51	annehmen, akzeptieren
according to 139	nach
accountant 55	Buchhalter(in)
accounts 26	Buchhaltung
acknowledge 148	bestätigen
acknowledgement 148	(Empfangs)bestätigung
act 44	vorspielen
actually 50	eigentlich, wirklich
addressed 133	adressiert, gerichtet an
advert 51	Anzeige, Inserat
advertise 114	bekannt machen
advertising leaflet 31	Werbeprospekt
advise 102	verständigen, Bescheid geben
afford 56	sich leisten
against 119; 138	gegen; gegenüber
age 12	Alter
agency 58	Vertretung
agenda 114	Tagesordnung
agent 59	Vertreter
aggressive 149	aggressiv
ago 23	vor
agree 55	übereinstimmen, zustimmen
air 40	Luft
air fare 107	Flugpreis
airline 61	Luftfahrtgesellschaft
airport 73	Flughafen
allow 33	erlauben, gestatten
alone 57	allein
although 149	obwohl
amazing 81	erstaunlich
amount 152	Summe, Betrag
anywhere 43	irgendwo
apologise 155	sich entschuldigen
application letter 51	Bewerbungsbrief, -schreiben
apply 147	gelten
appointment 38	Termin
area 95	Gegend
arm 82	Arm
arrange 72	arrangieren
arrangement 66	Absprache, Vorbereitung
as requested 135	wie gewünscht
as soon as possible 132	so schnell wie möglich
assistant 7	Assistent(in)
assume 152	annehmen
assure 150	versichern, zusichern
at sb's expense 107	auf Kosten, zu Lasten von
attend 118	teilnehmen an
auto(matic) 33	automatisch
autumn 81	Herbst
available 36	erhältlich, verfügbar

B

back 27	(Zug)ende
badly 150	sehr
bake 124	backen
bankrupt 57	bankrott
basic skills 54	Grundfertigkeiten
basis 152	Basis, Grundlage
beauty spot 114	hübsches/schönes Fleckchen (Erde)
because 17	weil
believe 63	glauben
belong 63	gehören
bent 110	verbogen
(With) best wishes 6	Alles Gute
between 20	zwischen
bicycle 40	Fahrrad
blank disk 30	leere Diskette
blind 34	Rollo, Jalousie
book 23	buchen, bestellen
book-keeping 54	Buchhaltung
bookshop 94	Buchhandlung
bracket 67	Klammer
branch 28	Filiale, Zweigstelle
break, broke, broken 27	brechen, kaputtmachen
breakdown 154	Panne
break down, broke, broken 27	zusammenbrechen
break out, broke, broken 27	ausbrechen
bridge 94	Brücke
British Consulate General 146	Britisches Generalkonsulat
brochure 36	Broschüre, Prospekt
build, built, built 114	bauen
build up, built, built 143	aufbauen
business 8	Geschäft, Firma

business, do ~ 8 ins Geschäft kommen
button 151 Knopf
button-hole 134 Knopfloch
buyer 136 Käufer(in), Einkäufer(in)

C

calculate 152 kalkulieren, berechnen
calculator 14 Taschenrechner
call up 57 aufrufen
caller 41 Anrufer
canteen 18 Kantine
capital city (pl -ies) 106 Hauptstadt
capital letters 35 Großbuchstaben
car maker 26 Autohersteller
careful 67 sorgfältig
case 112 Box
cash 135 Barzahlung
casserole 127 geschmortes Fleischgericht, Gulasch
cassette recorder 114 Kassettenrekorder
casualty (pl -ies) 23 Opfer
cat (catalogue) 22 Katalog
cause 153 verursachen
celebrate 123 feiern
certainly 51 sicherlich, gewiss
Chamber of Handelskammer
 Commerce 132
change 41 umwandeln
Channel Tunnel 23 Kanaltunnel
cheap 66 billig, günstig
check 11 überprüfen,
 kontrollieren
chemist's 95 Drogerie, Apotheke
cheque 156 Scheck
choice 56 Auswahl, ausgewählter
 Artikel
choose 40 wählen, aussuchen
church 94 Kirche
classroom 115 Klassenraum
clause 125 Satzteil
clear 114 klar
clerical worker 55 Schreib-, Bürokraft
clerk 10 Büroangestellte(r),
 kaufmännische(r)
 Angestellte(r)
click 35 klicken
clock 110 Uhr
club 119 Club
coast 65 Küste
coffee maker 34 Kaffeemaschine
colleague 8 Kollege, Kollegin

collection 68 Abholung
coloured 155 farbig
comfortable 66 bequem
comma 140 Komma
comment 110 Bemerkung,
 Kommentar
communicate 116 sich verständigen,
 kommunizieren
communication 146 Verständigung
community 114 Gemeinde
company 6 Gesellschaft, Firma
comparative 66 Steigerungsform des
 Adjektivs
compare 34 vergleichen
competition 153 Konkurrenz
complain 117 sich beklagen,
 beschweren
complaint 106 Reklamation
complete 6 vervollständigen
complex 64 kompliziert
complimentary Schlussformel, Gruß
 close 139
component 155 Bauelement, Einzelteil
comprehensive 133 Gesamt-
computerized 134 Computer-
concert 76 Konzert
conditions 10 Arbeitsbedingungen
conference 49 Konferenz
confirm 6 bestätigen
confirmation 145 Bestätigung
consider 126 in Erwägung ziehen,
 nachdenken über
consignment 135 Sendung
contact 49 Kontakt
contain 148 enthalten
container 107 Behälter, Container
contract 58 Vertrag
control system 27 Kontrollsystem
convenient 142 passend, günstig
conversation 19 Gespräch
cook 33 kochen
copy 31 Kopie, Zweitschrift;
 kopieren, abschreiben
corner 15 Ecke
correct 10 berichtigen,
 korrigieren
corridor 18 Gang, Flur
cost 136 Kosten
could 31 könnte
county (BE) 140 Grafschaft
couple 143 einige, ein paar
courier 64 Kurier

Alphabetisches Wörterverzeichnis

course *54* — Kurs, Lehrgang
cover *52* — zudecken, abdecken
cracked *110* — gesprungen
crash *27* — Zusammenstoß; zusammenstoßen
credit control *95* — Kreditabteilung
cross *23* — überqueren, durchqueren
current *132* — aktuell, letzte(r, s)
customer *27* — Kunde, Kundin

D

damage *27* — Schaden
date of birth *12* — Geburtsdatum
dated *136* — datiert
day off *33* — freier Tag
DDP (Delivered Duty Paid) *134* — Geliefert verzollt
deal with, *10* dealt, dealt — sich befassen mit, umgehen mit
decide *24* — (sich) entscheiden, sich entschließen
definitely *150* — bestimmt, sicher, genau
delay *150* — Verspätung
delete *31* — löschen
delighted *135* — sehr erfreut
deliver *136* — liefern
delivery (pl -ies) *23* — (Aus)lieferung
depart *101* — abfliegen
department *23* — Abteilung
describe *90* — beschreiben
description *110* — Beschreibung
design *26* — Design
desk *8* — Schreibtisch
desk lamp *14* — Schreibtischlampe
detail *22* — Einzelheit, Detail
develop *123* — entwickeln
diagram *111* — grafische Darstellung, Diagramm
diary *11* — Terminkalender
dictate *61* — diktieren
die *63* — sterben
difference *34* — Unterschied
different *10* — verschieden
direct sunlight *52* — direktes Sonnenlicht
direction *18* — Richtung
directly *141* — direkt
disconnect *52* — ausschalten, abstellen
discount *135* — Rabatt, Skonto
discuss *38* — besprechen
discussion *114* — Diskussion

dishwasher *56* — Geschirrspülmaschine
disk drive *30* — Diskettenlaufwerk
dislike *96* — nicht mögen
dispatch *23* — aufgeben, wegschicken
dissatisfied *154* — unzufrieden
distribution *18* — Vertrieb
do business *8* — ins Geschäft kommen
document *67* — Frachtpapier(e)
double *57* — doppelt
downstairs *19* — (nach) unten
draw *20* — zeichnen
drawer *15* — Schublade
drawing *139* — Zeichnung
drop *157* — Rückgang
due by *23* — fällig
dumpling *123* — Kloß, Knödel
during *86* — während

E

each *17* — jede(r, s)
early *17* — früh
economics *54* — Betriebswirtschaft
effect *153* — Wirkung, Auswirkung
eighth *52* — Achtel
either ... or *152* — entweder ... oder
emergency *23* — Notfall
empty *16* — leer
enclose *139* — beilegen
enclosure (enc.) *139* — Anlage
engaged *69* — besetzt
engine *143* — Motor
engineer *107* — Techniker(in)
enjoy *49* — gefallen
enough *52* — ausreichend, genug
enquiry *132* — Anfrage
envelope *11* — Briefumschlag
equip *146* — ausrüsten, ausstatten
equipment *14* — Ausstattung
especially *115* — besonders
etc. *110* — usw.
exact(ly) *23* — exakt, genau
exam *93* — Prüfung
excellent *107* — ausgezeichnet, hervorragend
except (for) *148* — außer
exception *135* — Ausnahme
exchange bureau *80* — Wechselstelle, Wechselstube
Excuse me. *7* — Entschuldigung.
expect *23* — erwarten, vermuten

expensive *8*	teuer	forward *155*	liefern, nachsenden
experience *49*	Erfahrung	free *39*	frei
explain *31*	erklären	freight forwarding agency *64*	Güterspedition
explanation *20*	Beschreibung		
express delivery company *68*	Expresslieferant, Kourierdienst	fresh line *35*	neue Zeile
		friendly *152*	freundlich
expression *28*	Ausdruck	further *135*	weitere(s, r)
extension ... *15*	Apparat ...	future *59*	Zukunft
extremely *154*	sehr		

G

		general *132*	allgemein
		get in touch with *150*	in Verbindung setzen
		girlfriend *83*	Freundin

F

facility *115*	Einrichtung, Möglichkeit	give back, gave, given *74*	zurückgeben
		glad *150*	froh
factory *7*	Fabrik, Werk	go dead, went, gone	ausfallen
fall through the floor *153*	in den Keller fallen	go out of business *58*	in Konkurs gehen
		Good afternoon. *8*	Guten Tag. (nachmittags)
fantastic *31*	fantastisch		
Far East *99*	Ferner Osten	good luck *81*	Viel Glück
far *82*	weit	goods *22*	Waren, Güter
fashion belt *155*	(modischer) Gürtel	government *114*	Regierung
favour *39*	Gefallen	graph *53*	Diagramm
fax machine *11*	Faxgerät	grateful *134*	dankbar
feature *31*	Merkmal, Kennzeichen	Great! *33*	Großartig!
ferry *23*	Fähre	greet *9*	(be)grüßen
few *8*	wenig, ein paar, wenige	greeting *144*	Gruß(formel)
field *49*	Bereich, Gebiet	grey *36*	grau
fight *114*	(be)kämpfen	ground floor *15*	Erdgeschoss
figure *26*	Zahl	grow, grew, grew *26*	wachsen
file *14*	Aktenordner	guess *125*	glauben, annehmen
filing *10*	Ablage	guys *(AE) 81*	Leute (umgangssprachlich)
fill in *144*	ausfüllen		
filling *123*	sättigend		
final *67*	endgültig		
finally *57*	schließlich	### H	
finance *18*	Finanzabteilung		
financial *156*	finanziell, wirtschaftlich	half *52*	Hälfte
firm *39*	Firma	handle *65*	erledigen, bearbeiten
fit *31*	passen	handwritten *144*	handgeschrieben
flat *56*	Wohnung	happen *40*	passieren, geschehen
fleet *146*	Fuhrpark	hard-working *49*	fleißig
flexible *54*	flexibel	hate *63*	hassen
flight *6*	Flug	haulage contractor *143*	Spedition, Transportunternehmen
flip chart *114*	Flip-chart		
flooding *150*	Überschwemmung	have pleasure in *147*	sich freuen
fly *31*	fliegen	head of the table *123*	Stirnseite des Tisches
follow *20*	folgen	head office *6*	Zentrale
following *22*	folgend(es, er)	heater *52*	Heizgerät
food *7*	Essen	heavy *33*	schwer
for the attention of *132*	zu Händen von	helpful *149*	hilfreich
form *17*	Form	herself *96*	sie selbst
formal(ly) *9; 144*	formell, förmlich		

Alphabetisches Wörterverzeichnis

hesitate *147*	zögern
high quality *137*	Qualitäts-
himself *96*	er selbst
hit *51*	schlagen
hold (the line) *69*	bleiben (am Apparat)
hold up, held, held *150*	aufhalten
hole punch *14*	Locher
hope *49*	hoffen
hot-house rose *64*	Treibhausrose
How do you do? *7*	Guten Tag/Abend!, Angenehm.
however *150*	jedoch, doch

I

idea *136*	Vorstellung
ideal *119*	ideal
identical *144*	identisch
ignore *152*	ignorieren
ill *33*	krank
illustration *30*	Zeichnung
immediate(ly) *67; 135*	sofort, umgehend
important *20*	wichtig
impossible *108*	unmöglich, undenkbar
improve *146*	verbessern
improvement *154*	Verbesserung
in charge *7*	verantwortlich sein
in fact *108*	tatsächlich, eigentlich
in the meantime *152*	in der Zwischenzeit
include *65*	einschließen
incomplete *151*	unvollständig
indeed *150*	tatsächlich
indication *146*	Angabe
industrial *132*	Industrie-
industry (pl -ies) *92*	Industrie
infinitive *25*	Grundform des Verbs
inform *108*	informieren, benachrichtigen
informal *7*	ungezwungen, nicht förmlich
information *132*	Auskunft, Information
initials *140*	Initialen, Anfangsbuchstaben
inside address *139*	Anschrift des Empfängers
inspection *151*	Kontrolle
instalment *153*	Rate
instead of *141*	anstatt
instruction *52*	Anweisung
interested in *133*	interessiert
interpreter *115*	Dolmetscher
interview *38*	Vorstellungsgespräch
introduce *9*	vorstellen, miteinander bekannt machen
introduction *144*	Einleitung, Einführung
invite *85*	einladen
invoice *152*	Rechnung
iron ore *64*	Eisenerz
item *32*	Artikel

J

jog *93*	joggen
join *26*	beginnen, Arbeit aufnehmen
journey *39*	Reise, Fahrt
just *7*	einfach

K

keep *31*	behalten
keep to *143*	einhalten
key in *31*	eingeben, einfügen
keyboard *30*	Tastatur
kind *134*	Art, Sorte
know, knew, known *15*	wissen

L

(un)labelled *34*	(nicht) beschriftet
ladies and gentlemen *123*	Meine Damen und Herren (Anrede)
land *83*	landen
lane *142*	Straße
last *126*	(an)dauern
laugh *31*	lachen
layout *139*	Layout
lead, led, led *157*	führen
leading *146*	führend
least *66*	wenigste(r, s), geringste(r, s)
lend *117*	leihen
length *68*	Länge
less *66*	weniger
less *137*	abzüglich
let's (let us) *7*	lassen Sie uns
letterhead *133*	Briefkopf
lie *63*	liegen
lift *18*	Fahrstuhl
lightning, in case of ~ *52*	bei Blitzgefahr
light unit *107*	Lampe, Leuchte
link *126*	Verbindung
live *9*	wohnen
load *67*	beladen
local *28*	örtlich

look after *9*	betreuen	mention *147*	erwähnen
look around *7*	ansehen, umsehen	menu *35*	Menü
look forward to *132*	sich freuen auf	method *65*	Methode, Verfahren
lorry *144*	Lastwagen, LKW	microphone *30*	Mikrofon
lose *35*	verlieren	midday *23*	Mittag, mittags
loud *67*	laut	mind *93*	jdm. etwas ausmachen
loudspeaker *114*	Lautsprecher	mislay, -laid, -laid *152*	verlegen
low *117*	niedrig	missing *9*	fehlend
lower *136*	niedriger	model letter *156*	Beispielbrief
Ltd. (Limited) *7*	GmbH	modem *154*	Modem
lucky, be ~ *23*	Glück haben	modernize *134*	modernisieren
luggage *80*	Gepäck	monitor *30*	Monitor, Bildschirm
lunchtime *65*	Mittagszeit	monthly *17*	monatlich
luxury *157*	Luxus-	motorbike *83*	Motorrad
		motorway *67*	Autobahn
		mouse pad *30*	Mausunterlage, Mouse Pad
M		move *26*	wechseln
M.D. (managing director) *18*	Geschäftsführer(in)	mushroom *124*	Champignon
magic *31*	Zauberei	myself *33*	selbst
mail *10*	Post, mit der Post schicken		
mailroom supervisor *10*	Poststellenleiter(in)	**N**	
		narrow *117*	schmal
make *139*	(Marken)produkt, Marke	near *9*	bei, nahe
make sure *23*	absichern, sicherstellen	nearly *12*	beinahe, fast
manage *93*	schaffen	necessary *25*	nötig, notwendig
manufactured *139*	hergestellt, angefertigt	negative *21*	Verneinung
manufacturer *64*	Hersteller	neither *118*	keine
manufacturing *43*	Herstellung, Produktion	next to *18*	neben
map *81*	Wegskizze, Stadtplan	nobody *73*	niemand
marine *119*	Meeres-	none *108*	keine (r, s)
mark *20*	markieren	not possibly *153*	unmöglich
market *52*	Markt	note *28*	Notiz
marketing *12*	Marketing	notepad *14*	Notizblock
married *141*	verheiratet	notification *143*	Benachrichtigung
match *8*	zuordnen		
material *23*	Material, Stoff		
maternity leave *41*	Mutterschaftsurlaub		
matter *91*	Angelegenheit	**O**	
matter, It doesn't ~. *23*	Es ist egal.	o'clock *11*	volle Stunde, um ... Uhr
meal *51*	Essen	obvious *148*	offensichtlich
mean *54*	bedeuten	of course *39*	natürlich, selbstverständlich
meaning *40*	Bedeutung, Sinn	offer *135*	Angebot; anbieten
meat dish *123*	Fleischgericht	offering help *62*	Hilfe anbieten
mechanical *150*	mechanisch, technisch	office administration *54*	Büroorganisation
meet, met, met *9*	(sich) treffen	office furniture *7*	Büromöbel
meeting *39*	Besprechung, Sitzung	office services *18*	Büroservice, zentraler Dienst
meeting room *18*	Besprechungsraum		
member *77*	Mitglied	on departure *148*	bei Abfahrt
memo *19*	Notiz, Merkzettel	on foot *82*	zu Fuß
mend *83*	reparieren		

Alphabetisches Wörterverzeichnis

on receipt *135*   nach Erhalt
on-screen *31*   direkt am Bildschirm
operation *43*   Filiale
opposite *18*   gegenüber
order *11*   bestellen
organization *7*   Unternehmen
organization chart *26*   Organisationsübersicht
organize *96*   organisieren
original *139*   original
outside *91*   außerhalb
outstanding *152*   ausstehend
oven *124*   Backofen
over there *7*   da drüben
overdue *152*   überfällig
overhead projector *114*   Tageslichtprojektor, Overheadprojektor
overlook *156*   übersehen
oversight *151*   Versehen

P

pack *74*   packen
package *68*   Paket
packaging department *151*   Verpackungsabteilung
paper clip *14*   Büroklammer
paperwork *93*   Schreibarbeit
paragraph *67*   Absatz, Abschnitt
participant *120*   Teilnehmer(in)
particularly *157*   besonders
pass (an exam) *108*   bestehen
pass *133*   weiterleiten
passenger *77*   Passagier, Fluggast
passport *58*   Reisepass
pay *10*   Lohn, Gehalt
pay cheque *17*   Gehaltsscheck, -zahlung
payable *152*   zahlbar
payment *135*   Bezahlung
per cent *138*   Prozent
perhaps *8*   vielleicht
personnel *7*   Personal
personnel manager *6*   Personalleiter(in)
petrol tank *27*   (Benzin)tank
phone, be on the ~ *23*   telefonieren
phone call *57*   Anruf
photocopier *51*   Fotokopierer
phrase *9*   Ausdruck, Redewendung
pick up (telephone) *61*   abnehmen
pick up *16*   aufheben, hochheben
pie chart *52*   Kreisdiagramm
place *157*   erteilen

plan *36*   planen, vorhaben
plan of action *114*   Plan
plastic *151*   Plastik
Pleased to meet you. *7*   Es freut mich, Sie kennen zu lernen.
point, no ~ in ... *93*   keinen Zweck haben
polite *117*   höflich
popular *127*   beliebt
pork *123*   Schweinefleisch
position *12*   Stellung, Position
poster *114*   Plakat
power cable *30*   Stromkabel
practical *66*   praktisch, realistisch
practise *8*   üben
prepare *20*   vorbereiten
present *74*   Geschenk
presentation *115*   Vorführung, Präsentation
press *31*   drücken
pretty *54*   ziemlich, ganz
previously *72*   vorher
price *135*   Preis
price list *132*   Preisliste
price war *153*   Preiskrieg
print out *31*   (aus)drucken
printer *30*   Drucker
probably *49*   wahrscheinlich
procedure *151*   Verfahren
produce *81*   produzieren, herstellen
producer *7*   Produzent, Hersteller
product *8*   Produkt, Erzeugnis
product planning *26*   Produktplanung
production manager *7*   Produktionsleiter(in)
programmer *55*   Programmierer(in)
progress *126*   Fortschritt
project *123*   Projekt
promise *57*   versprechen
prompt *134*   sofort, prompt
properly *109*   richtig, korrekt
public *114*   öffentlich
punctuation *140*   Zeichensetzung, Interpunktion
purchasing *12*   Einkauf
put in order *11*   in richtiger Reihenfolge ordnen

Q

qty (quantity) *22*   Menge, Quantität
quarter *52*   Viertel
quite *7*   ziemlich, ganz
quotation *134*   Kostenvoranschlag
quote *134*   nennen, angeben

R

R&D (research and development) *18* — Forschung und Entwicklung
rail *40* — Zug
railway *94* — Eisenbahn
raise *124* — erheben
range *31* — Sortiment
rapidly *53* — schnell
rare *139* — selten
rather *69* — ziemlich, ganz
raw materials *111* — Rohstoffe
reach *20* — erreichen
real *31* — echt
really *26* — wirklich, eigentlich
reason *114* — Grund
receive *132* — erhalten, bekommen
recent *53* — letzte(r,s)
recently *28* — neulich, kürzlich
reception *18* — Rezeption, Empfang
receptionist *10* — Herr/Dame am Empfang
recession *156* — Rezession
recommend *124* — empfehlen
record card *12* — Karteikarte
reference number *57* — Aktenzeichen, Kennziffer
regards *99* — Gruß
registered *140* — eingetragen, eingeschrieben
regret *108* — bedauern
relationship *143* — Beziehung
reliable *67* — zuverlässig
remain *53* — bleiben
remaining *135* — übrig, restlich
remember *48* — sich erinnern
reminder *152* — Mahnung
repair *51* — reparieren
repeat *41* — wiederholen
reply *134* — Antwort
report *10* — Bericht
reporter *126* — Reporter(in)
representative (rep) *33* — (Handels-)Vertreter(in)
require *135* — benötigen
reservation *84* — Reservierung
responsible, be ~ for *23* — verantwortlich sein
responsibility (pl -ies) *91* — Tätigkeit, Verantwortlichkeit
rest *51* — Pause
result *82* — Ergebnis
retail *153* — Einzelhandel
retailer *146* — Einzelhändler(in)
return *72* — Rückkehr; zurückkehren
rewrite *117* — umschreiben
rich *125* — ergiebig
ring, rang, rung *91* — läuten, klingeln
rise, rose, risen *53* — ansteigen
risk *93* — riskieren
roadworks *67* — Straßenbauarbeiten
role *127* — Rolle
route *65* — Route, Strecke
ruler *14* — Lineal
run *7* — leiten, führen
run out of *140* — ausgehen, alle werden

S

salary *92* — Gehalt
sales office *7* — Verkaufsbüro
sales representative *27* — (Handels-)Vertreter(in)
salesperson *128* — Verkäufer(in)
salutation *139* — Anrede
same *12* — gleiche(r, s), der-, die-, dasselbe
satisfied *137* — zufrieden
schedule *65* — Zeitplan
scratched *110* — zerkratzt
sea *40* — Meer
secret *64* — geheim
secretary *10* — Sekretär(in)
section *49* — Abteilung
seem *27* — scheinen
select *35* — auswählen
sell *8* — verkaufen
seller *136* — Verkäufer(in)
senior accountant *26* — leitende(r) Buchhalter(in)
separate *140* — getrennt
serious *156* — ernst
set *31* — einstellen
settle *153* — begleichen
sewing machine *132* — Nähmaschine
sheet *143* — Seite, Blatt
shelf *36* — Aufsatz
ship *40* — Schiff
shipment *65* — Schiffsladung
shipping document *111* — Frachtpapiere
shock, be in ~ *23* — schockiert sein
shopping *59* — Einkauf
shortly *148* — in Kürze
shout *57* — rufen
show round *39* — herumführen

Alphabetisches Wörterverzeichnis

shower *51* — Dusche
sightseeing *91* — Besichtigung, Stadtbesichtigung
sign *69* — unterschreiben
signature block *139* — Unterschriftsabschnitt
simply *144* — einfach
since *84* — seit
single ticket *77* — einfache Fahrkarte
situation *82* — Situation
size *36* — Maße
ski *93* — Ski laufen
slide projector *114* — Diaprojektor
sliding shelf *36* — Auszug
slot *115* — (Programm)abschnitt
slow down *67* — aufhalten
smile *23* — lächeln
snack *51* — Imbiss
software pack *134* — Softwarepaket
solar cell *112* — Solarzelle
solve *108* — lösen
sound *81* — klingen
soup *124* — Suppe
south *67* — nach Süden, südlich
space *31* — Leerraum
spare part *32* — Ersatzteil
special *31* — besondere(r,s), Sonder-
specialist *54* — Spezialist(in)
specially *139* — speziell, extra
specific *134* — speziell
spell *57* — buchstabieren
spelling code *61* — Buchstabiercode
spelling mistake *51* — (Recht)schreibfehler
spend, spent, spent *75* — ausgeben
spoken *144* — gesprochen
sports centre *94* — Sportzentrum
staff *10* — Personal, Mitarbeiter
stairs *18* — Treppe
standard *107* — Norm
staple *14* — Heftklammer
stapler *14* — Hefter
starter *124* — Vorspeise
statement *21* — Aussage
stationery cupboard *11* — Schrank für Büromaterial
steel *22* — Stahl
steelworks *64* — Stahlwerk
step *123* — Schritt
still *9* — noch
stock level *111* — Warenbestand
stock list *57* — Warenliste
stop *98* — Aufenthalt, Zwischenlandung
store *11* — Lager
straight ahead *84* — geradeaus
study *31* — Arbeitszimmer
style *108* — Schnitt, Art
subject *128* — Thema, Fachgebiet
subject line *139* — Betreff
submit *138* — unterbreiten
successful *50* — erfolgreich
such *136* — solche(r,s)
suffer *157* — leiden
sugar *39* — Zucker
suggest *40* — vorschlagen
suggestion *104* — Vorschlag
suit *104* — passen
suitcase *80* — Koffer
superlative *66* — höchste Steigerungsform des Adjektivs
supplier *23* — Anbieter
supply *22* — (be)liefern
suppose *65* — glauben, annehmen
surprise *72* — Überraschung
survey *56* — Umfrage
switch *75* — Schalter

T

table *53* — Tabelle
take *100* — dauern
take a seat *41* — Platz nehmen
take/leave a message *62* — etwas ausrichten / Nachricht hinterlassen
talent *123* — Talent, Begabung
talented *125* — begabt, talentiert
taste *39* — schmecken
tasty *123* — schmackhaft
taxi-rank *84* — Taxistand
technical school *28* — Gewerbeschule
tell *7* — sagen
term *134* — Bedingung
terminal *78* — Endstation
terrible *57* — schrecklich, fürchterlich
right, That's ~. *7* — Das stimmt.
theatre *83* — Theater
therefore *153* — deshalb
third *52* — Drittel
though *100* — doch, tatsächlich
three quarters *52* — drei Viertel
three times a week *11* — dreimal pro Woche
tick *128* — abhaken
tidy *34* — ordentlich, aufgeräumt
timetable *78* — Fahrplan
tired *51* — müde

tiring *124*	anstrengend, ermüdend	
title *48*	Bezeichnung	
together *11*	zusammen	
tomato (pl -es) *124*	Tomate	
ton *22*	Tonne	
tool *38*	Werkzeug	
total *22*	Endsumme, Gesamtpreis	
tough *153*	hart	
tour *98*	Tour, Rundfahrt	
tourist information office *94*	Touristeninformationsbüro	
towards *67*	auf … zu, in Richtung	
trade fair *8*	Handelsmesse	
traditional *91*	traditionell	
traffic *67*	Verkehr	
traffic lights *94*	Ampel	
train *26*	eine (Berufs)ausbildung machen, ausbilden	
trainee *6*	Auszubildende(r)	
training *26*	Ausbildungsabteilung	
translator *115*	Übersetzer(in)	
transmit *144*	übertragen	
transport *151*	transportieren	
tray *34*	Ablage(korb)	
trip (back) *73*	(Rück-)reise, -fahrt	
trouble *146*	Mühe	
truck *23*	Lastkraftwagen	
true *30*	richtig	
try *23*	probieren, versuchen	
turn *23*	(sich) drehen	
turn down *67*	leiser stellen	
twin-bed *119*	Zweibett-	
two thirds *52*	zwei Drittel	
type *10*	tippen, eingeben	

U

undamaged *145*	unbeschädigt
unfortunately *149*	leider
unit price *22*	Stückpreis
unsatisfactory *108*	unbefriedigend, nicht zufriedenstellend
untidy *34*	unordentlich, unaufgeräumt
until *28*	bis
upstairs *19*	(nach) oben
urgent *22*	dringend
use *9*	benutzen, verwenden
useful *49*	nützlich
user's handbook *30*	Benutzerhandbuch
usual *39*	gewöhnlich
usually *11*	normalerweise

V

valid *57*	gültig
value *22*	Wert
van *64*	Lieferwagen, Transporter
various *11*	verschiedene
VAT (Value Added Tax) *140*	Mehrwertsteuer
veal *123*	Kalbfleisch
vegetarian *120*	Vegetarier(in)
via *23*	durch, über
video camera *114*	Videokamera
video recorder *56*	Videorecorder
view *119*	Blick, Ausblick

W

warehouse *91*	Lager
washing machine *56*	Waschmaschine
waste of time *93*	Zeitverschwendung
wastepaper bin *14*	Papierkorb
weigh *68*	wiegen
welcome *10*	begrüßen, empfangen
whether *141*	ob
while *20*	während
white board *114*	White Board
wholesaler *149*	Großhändler(in)
wide *117*	breit
willing *135*	gewillt sein
wine *124*	Wein
wish *63*	wünschen
within *135*	innerhalb
wordprocessing *31*	Textverarbeitung
workplace *20*	Arbeitsplatz
worried *150*	besorgt, beunruhigt
worry *49*	sich Sorgen machen
worse, worst *71*	schlechter, am schlechtesten
worth, it's ~ *91*	wert sein, sich lohnen
would you like … *39*	möchten Sie …

Y

yet *73*	schon, bereits
you're welcome *39*	nichts zu danken
yours faithfully *132*	Hochachtungsvoll, Mit freundlichem Gruß
yours sincerely *134*	Mit freundlichem Gruß
yourself *28*	sich selbst

Z

ZIP code (AE) *140*	Postleitzahl
zip-fastener *151*	Reißverschluss

Grundwortschatz

Diese Liste enthält ca. 400 Grundwörter, die bei ihrem ersten Auftreten im Kurs als bekannt vorausgesetzt werden.

A

a lot	viele
a, an	ein(e)
about	über, wegen
above	über, oberhalb von
across	(hin, her)über
add	hinzufügen, beitragen
address	Adresse
afraid, be ~	befürchten
again	wieder, nochmals
airport	Flughafen
all	alle
along	entlang
already	schon
also	auch
always	immer
and	und
angry with	böse auf
another	noch eine(r, s)
answer	beantworten; Antwort
any	irgendein
are	sind
arrival	Ankunft
arrive	ankommen
as	als, wie
ask	fragen
at	an
away	weg

B

bad	schlecht
bag	Tasche, Beutel
bank	Bank
bath	Bad
be, was/were, been	sein
beautiful	schön
become, became, become	werden
bed	Bett
before	vor, vorher
begin, began, begun	anfangen, beginnen
beginner	Anfänger(in)
below	unter, unterhalb
best	beste(r, s)
better	besser
big	groß
biro	Kugelschreiber
birthday	Geburtstag
bit	Stück, wenig
black	schwarz
boat	Boot
book	Buch
boss	Chef(in)
bottle	Flasche
box	Kasten, Büchse
break	Pause
breakfast	Frühstück
bring, brought, brought	bringen
brother	Bruder
brown	braun
bus	Bus
busy	beschäftigt
but	aber
buy, bought, bought	kaufen
by	von, durch, mit
bye	tschüss

C

call	(an)rufen
can, could	können
cannot	nicht können
car	Auto
carry	tragen, bringen
cartoon	Karikatur, Cartoon
catch, caught, caught	fangen, erwischen
chair	Stuhl
cheap	billig
child, children	Kind, Kinder
cinema	Kino
class	Klasse
clean	sauber
close	schließen
clothes (pl)	Kleider, Kleidung
clothing	Bekleidung
coffee	Kaffee
colleague	Kollege, Kollegin
colour	Farbe
come, came, come	kommen
computer	Computer
constant	dauernd, konstant
cost, cost, cost	kosten; Kosten
country (pl -ies)	Land (Länder)
cup	Tasse

D

day	Tag
Dear ...	Liebe(s, r)...
deep	tief
dialogue	Dialog
difficult	schwierig
dinner	Mittagsmahlzeit, Abendessen
dirty	schmutzig
do, did, done	tun, machen
door	Tür
drink, drank, drunk	trinken
drive, drove, driven	fahren

E

eat, ate, eaten	essen
end	Ende, beenden
evening	Abend
every	jede(s, r)
everybody	jedermann

everything	alles
exercise	Übung
export	Export, Ausfuhr
extra	extra, zusätzlich

F

face	Gesicht
fall, fell, fallen	fallen; Sturz
family (pl -ies)	Familie
fast	schnell
father	Vater
feel, felt, felt	fühlen
film	Film
find, found, found	finden
fine	schön
finish	beenden; Ende
fire	Feuer
first	erste(s, r), zuerst
fish	Fisch
floor	Fußboden, Stockwerk
football	Fußball
for	für
for example	zum Beispiel
forget, forgot, forgotten	vergessen
friend	Freund(in)
from	von
full	voll

G

game	Spiel
get, got, got	bekommen, werden
give, gave, given	geben
glass	Glas
go, went, gone	gehen
gold	Gold
good morning	Guten Morgen
goodbye	Auf Wiedersehen
group	Gruppe

H

happy	glücklich
has, have, had, had	hat, haben
he	er
hear, heard, heard	hören
hello	Hallo
help	helfen; Hilfe
her	sie, ihr, ihre(s, r),
here	hier
high	hoch
him	ihn, ihm
his	sein, seine(r, s)
holiday	Ferien, Urlaub
home, go ~	Heim, Heimat (nach Hause)
homework	Hausaufgaben
hotel	Hotel
hour	Stunde
hungry	hungrig

I

I	ich
ice-cream	Eiskrem
if	wenn, falls, ob
import	Import, Einfuhr
in	in
information	Information
intelligent	intelligent
interesting	interessant
international	international
into	in ... hinein
is	ist

J

job	Aufgabe, Beruf

K

kilo(gram)	Kilo(gramm)
kilometre	Kilometer
kitchen	Küche

L

language	Sprache
large	groß, weit
last	letzte(s, r), dauern
late	spät, verspätet
learn, learnt, learned	lernen
learner	Lernende(r)
leave, left, left	(ver)lassen
left	links
letter	Brief
life	Leben
like	mögen, ähnlich wie
list	auflisten; Liste
listen	zuhören
little	klein
(a) little	ein wenig
long	lang
look	sehen
love	lieben; Liebe
lunch	Mittagessen

M

machine	Maschine
make, made, made	machen
manager	Geschäftsführer(in)
many	viele
maximum	Maximum
metre	Meter
middle	Mitte
milk	Milch
minimum	Minimum
minute	Minute
mistake	Fehler
moment	Moment, Augenblick
money	Geld
month	Monat
more	mehr
morning	Morgen
most	die meisten
mother	Mutter
Mr	Herr (Anrede)

Grundwortschatz

Mrs	Frau (Anrede)	per	pro	see,	sehen
much	viel	person	Person	saw,	
music	Musik	phone	telefonieren;	seen	
must	müssen		Telefon	send,	schicken, senden
my	meine(s, r)	photo(graph)	fotografieren; Foto	sent, sent	
		picture	Bild	sentence	Satz
N		pizza	Pizza	set,	setzen, stellen;
name	Name	place	platzieren; Stelle, Platz,	set, set	Satz, Reihe
need	brauchen	plan	planen; Plan	she	sie
new	neu	plane	Flugzeug	shoe	Schuh
news	Nachricht(en)	play	spielen	shop	einkaufen;
newspaper	Zeitung	please	bitte		Geschäft, Laden
next	nächste(s, r)	police	Polizei	short	kurz
nice	nett	post	abschicken	should	sollte
night	Nacht	post office	Postamt	show,	zeigen; Schau
no	nein	problem	Problem	showed, shown	
not	nicht	put,	setzen, stellen, legen	shut, shut, shut	schließen
now	jetzt, nun	put, put			
number (no.)	Nummer, (An)zahl			sister	Schwester
		Q		sit, sat, sat	sitzen
O		question	Frage	sleep, slept, slept	schlafen
object	Gegenstand	quick	schnell		
of	von	quiet	leise, still	slow	langsam
office	Büro			small	klein
old	alt	**R**		smoke	rauchen
on	auf	radio	Radio	so	so
one	eins	read, read, read	lesen	some	einige, etwas
only	nur			somebody	jemand
onto	auf, an	ready	fertig, bereit	someone else	noch jemand
open	offen, öffnen	red	rot	something	etwas
or	oder	restaurant	Restaurant, Gaststätte	sometimes	manchmal
other	andere(s, r)			soon	bald
		right	richtig, rechts	sorry	Entschuldigung!
P		river	Fluss	space	(Leer)raum, Lücke
page	Seite	road	Straße		
paper	Papier	room	Zimmer, Raum	speak	sprechen
parents	Eltern	run, ran, run	rennen, laufen	spoke, spoken	
park	Park			speaker	Sprecher(in), Redner(in)
part	Teil				
partner	Partner(in)	**S**		speed	Geschwindigkeit
party	Party, Feier	say, said, said	sagen	start	beginnen, starten
past	Vergangenheit			station	Bahnhof
pay, paid, paid	bezahlen			stay	bleiben
pen	Füller				
pencil	Bleistift				
people	Leute, Menschen				

stop	aufhören, anhalten	to	zu	with	mit
street	Straße	today	heute	without	ohne
strong	stark	tomorrow	morgen	woman, women	Frau, Frauen
student	Student	tonight	heute Abend	wonderful	wunderbar
stupid	dumm	too	auch	word	Wort
supermarket	Supermarkt	top	Spitze, Gipfel	work	arbeiten; Arbeit
supper	Abendessen	town	Stadt	worker	Arbeiter(in)
swim, swam, swum	schwimmen	train	Zug	write, wrote, written	schreiben
		translate	übersetzen		
		translation	Übersetzung	writer	Schriftsteller(in)
		transport	transportieren; Transport	wrong	falsch

T

take, took, taken	nehmen				

U

talk	reden, sprechen; Vortrag	under	unter		
		understand, understood, understood	verstehen		
taxi	Taxi				
tea	Tee				
teach, taught, taught	lehren			Y	
				year	Jahr
		V		yes	ja
team	Mannschaft	very	sehr	yesterday	gestern
telephone	Telefon	visit	besuchen; Besuch	you	du, Sie, ihr
television (TV)	Fernsehen			young	jung
		visitor	Besucher	your	dein(e), Ihr(e), eure, euer
tell, told, told	erzählen			yours	deins, Ihr(e)s, eures
tennis	Tennis	W			
test	testen; Test	wait	warten		
text	Text	walk	(zu Fuß) gehen		
than	als	want	wollen		
thank	danken	wash	waschen		
Thanks, Thank you	Danke	watch	schauen, beobachten; Armbanduhr		
the	der, die, das	water	Wasser		
their	ihr (Mehrzahl)	way	Weg		
them	sie, ihnen	we	wir		
then	dann	weather	Wetter		
these	diese	week	Woche		
they	sie (Mehrzahl)	weekend	Wochenende		
thing	Ding, Sache	what	was		
think	denken	when	wann		
thirsty	durstig	where	wo		
this	dies	which	welche(s, r)		
those	solche	who	wer		
through	durch	why	warum		
ticket	Fahrkarte	will	wird, werden; Willen		
time	Zeit, Uhrzeit	window	Fenster		
		winter	Winter		

Ortsnamen

America [əˈmerɪkə]
American [əˈmerɪkən]
Amsterdam [ˈæmstədæm]
Antwerp [ˈæntwɜːp]
Asia [ˈeɪʃə]
Australia [ɒˈstreɪlɪə]
Barcelona [ˌbɑːsɪˈləʊnə]
Birmingham [ˈbɜːmɪŋəm]
Bradford [ˈbrædfəd]
Brazilia [brəˈzɪlɪə]
Brisbane [ˈbrɪzbən]
Bristol [ˈbrɪstl]
Britain [ˈbrɪtn]
British [ˈbrɪtɪʃ]
Cairns [keənz]
Calais [ˈkæleɪ]
Canada [ˈkænədə]
Canadian [kəˈneɪdɪən]
Cologne [kəˈləʊn]
Denmark [ˈdenmɑːk]
Dover [ˈdəʊvə]
Dublin [ˈdʌblɪn]
England [ˈɪŋglənd]
English [ˈɪŋglɪʃ]
Europe [ˈjʊərəp]
European [ˌjʊərəˈpɪən]
Felixstowe [ˈfiːlɪkstəʊ]
France [frɑːns]
French [ˌfrentʃ]
Frederikshavn [ˈfredrɪkshɑːvn]
Gatwick [ˈgætwɪk]
Germany [ˈdʒɜːmənɪ]
German [ˌdʒɜːmən]
Glasgow [ˈglɑːzgəʊ]
Göteborg [gœtəbɔːg]

Hamburg [ˈhæmbɜːg]
Heathrow [ˌhiːˈθrəʊ]
Holland [ˈhɒlənd]
Hong Kong [ˌhɒŋ ˈkɒŋ]
Indonesia [ˌɪndəʊˈniːzɪə]
Ipswich [ˈɪpswɪtʃ]
Ireland [ˈaɪələnd]
Israel [ˈɪzreɪl]
Italian [ɪˈtæljən]
Japan [dʒəˈpæn]
Japanese [ˌdʒæpəˈniːz]
Kensington [ˈkenzɪŋtən]
Korea [kəˈrɪə]
London [ˈlʌndən]
Los Angeles [lɒsˈændʒəliːz]
Manchester [ˈmæntʃɪstə]
Manhattan [mænˈhætn]
Melbourne [ˈmelbən]
Mexico [ˈmeksɪkəʊ]
Milan [mɪˈlæn]
Moscow [ˈmɒskəʊ]
Munich [ˈmjuːnɪk]
New York [njuːˈjɔːk]
Norfolk [ˈnɔːfək]
Nuremberg [ˈnjʊərəmbɜːg]
Örebro [ˈœrebruː]
Osaka [əʊˈsɑːkə]
Ostend [ɒstˈend]
Ottawa [ˈɒtəwə]
Oxford [ˈɒksfəd]
Paris [ˈpærɪs]
Perth [pɜːθ]
Portsmouth [ˈpɔːtsməθ]
Romford [ˈrɒmfəd]
Seoul [səʊl]

Singapore [sɪŋəˈpɔː]
Spain [speɪn]
Spanish [ˈspænɪʃ]
Stockholm [ˈstɒkhəʊm]
Sweden [ˈswiːdn]
Swedish [ˈswiːdɪʃ]
Switzerland [ˈswɪtsələnd]
Sydney [ˈsɪdni]
Tenerife [ˌtenəˈriːf]
Thai [taɪ]
Tokyo [ˈtəʊkɪəʊ]
Toulouse [tuːˈluːz]
Trelleborg [ˈtreləbɔːg]
United Kingdom (UK)
[juːˌnaɪtɪd ˈkɪŋdəm]
Wales [weɪlz]

BILDNACHWEIS

James Abram, *Salzburg*	S. 106
J. Allan Cash, *London*	S. 23, 119 (2)
Comstock, *Berlin*	Titelbild
dpa Fotoreport, *Frankfurt/M.*	S. 106 (2)
David Graham, *London*	S. 6, 7 (3), 10, 11, 12 (2), 14, 15 (2), 23, 26 (2), 27, 30 (6), 31, 35, 38 (2), 39 (2), 48 (4), 54 (2), 56 (2), 65, 68 (3), 72, 73, 81, 91 (2), 107 (2), 124
The Image Bank, *Berlin*	S. 56, 106 (2)
Keystone, *Hamburg*	S. 22, 56
Barbara Köpke, *Berlin*	S. 48
Helga Lade Fotoagentur, *Berlin*	S. 56 (3), 122 (5)
Susanne Schütz, *Berlin*	S. 48